English Catholic Modernism

English Catholic Modernism

MAUDE PETRE'S WAY OF FAITH

Clyde F. Crews

UNIVERSITY OF NOTRE DAME PRESS
BURNS & OATES

First published 1984 by
University of Notre Dame Press
Notre Dame, Indiana 46556 USA

in association with

Burns & Oates
Wellwood, North Farm Road,
Tunbridge Wells, Kent, TN2 3DR, England

Library of Congress Cataloging in Publication Data

Crews, Clyde F.
  English Catholic modernism.

  Bibliography: p. 137.
  Includes index.
  1. Petre, Maude Dominica, 1863-1942.   2. Catholics—
England—Biography.   3. Modernism—Catholic Church—
England.   I. Title.
BX705.P438C73   1983   230'.2'0924   [B]   83-50747
ISBN 0-268-00912-0 (US)
ISBN 086012 136 4 (UK)

Manufactured in the United States of America

To All the Gang at 634—
My Old Kentucky Home

Publication of this volume
is assisted by a grant from the
Catholic Theological Society of America

Contents

Foreword

WHEN INQUISITIVE FRIENDS asked Lady Lindsay what her young niece, Maude Petre, was doing in Rome, she replied: "Maude has gone to Rome to study for the priesthood." Actually, she was studying Thomistic philosophy and theology with a tutor. This was in 1885 when the stage was being set for "Modernism," which was to become a minority movement during a twenty-year period, from 1890 to 1910, in England, France and Italy. Modernism was inspired by a legitimate desire of the Church to proclaim the Christian faith to each new generation in an adequate manner. In this it foreshadowed the Second Vatican Council. Karl Rahner and Herbert Vorgrimler expressed it well when they wrote: "Modernism simply proposed wrong solutions to many problems it had grasped aright." They concluded their remarks with the sad commentary: "To this day Modernism unfortunately remains a term used for spiteful invective by arrogant people in the Church who have no idea how difficult faith is for men [and women] of our time."

But who was Maude Dominica Petre and how does she fit into the picture of "Modernism"? The Jesuit, George Tyrrell, and Baron Friedrich von Hügel are well enough known as the most prominent characters in the drama which unfolded in England at the beginning of the twentieth century. In France, of course, Alfred Loisy and Henri Bremond (also a Jesuit) were already making their mark. It is curious that so little is known of Maude Petre's involvement, except in her relations with George Tyrrell, whose autobiography she published posthumously. To a lesser extent she collaborated with Bremond and von Hügel. Doubtless the reason for her relative obscurity is due to the fact that a complete life and study of her writings has not up to now been published.

It is therefore an important publishing event to have Father Clyde Crews' carefully researched and documented work make its appearance. Maude Petre was a "valiant woman" of the Church, whose main fault was to have been born a century ahead of her time. We can look to her as an example of one who held firmly to her convictions despite official disapproval. Through countless trials and sufferings, which this book records dispassionately, she continued her personal journey remaining faithful to Christ and His Church.

As was the case with so many others whose creative and pioneering work was held suspect by overzealous guardians of the faith, history vindicated Maude Petre, especially with the Second Vatican Council. Her witness should be a source of encouragement for women today who must struggle to make themselves heard, both inside and outside the Church. If evidence were still needed, this book makes it abundantly clear how valuable and essential are the feminine insights of philosophical and theological reflection. I heartily recommend this book on Maude Petre, and I hope it will reach the wide audience it rightly deserves.

Brother Patrick Hart
Abbey of Gethsemani

Acknowledgments

AT FORDHAM UNIVERSITY, it was Dr. John Heaney who first mentioned the name Maude Petre to me and encouraged this research. Father James J. Hennesey, S.J., did some encouraging of his own and mentored the project in its first incarnation as a doctoral dissertation. Msgr. E. Harold Smith of New York provided much of the emotional mentoring of the piece.

In England, the family of Miss Petre were particularly helpful. In this respect I must specially mention her niece, Mrs. Maurice Pirenne of Oxford. Special thanks are also due to MDP's friends in England, Cally Merewether, Antonia White, and that dean of British Modernist studies, Dr. Alec Vidler. In France, Madame Anne Louise-David proved to be extraordinarily helpful.

For encouragement to publish, I wholeheartedly thank Brother Patrick Hart, O.C.S.O., of the Abbey of Gethsemani, Sister Mary Luke Tobin of the Sisters of Loretto, Dr. Ellen Leonard, C.S.J., of the University of Toronto, and Dr. Thomas O'Meara, O.P., of Notre Dame University. At Spalding College, Sister Mary Michael Creamer of the Sisters of Charity of Nazareth was of great assistance in proofreading the manuscript. At the University of Notre Dame Press, Ann Rice proved to be a superior editor.

Down south in Louisville, Dr. Kathleen Lyons of Bellarmine College and my brother Stevens both gave the original manuscript careful editorial and proofreading scrutiny. Given a most pressing original deadline, the support skills and services of Clara and Marynell Quill and of Hanna and Allan Steinberg were indispensable. And in the original work as well as in the reincarnation as a second manuscript, it was my mother, Nell Crews, the professional typist par excellence, who turned first draft chaos into the dignity of the printed page.

Introduction:

MAUDE PETRE AND THE ENGLISH CATHOLIC TRADITION

To speak of English Modernism in the Roman Catholic Church is generally to speak of George Tyrrell and Friedrich von Hügel, quite rightly regarded as pivotal thinkers around whom that religious movement turned in the early years of this century. There is, however, another figure whom major critical historians of Modernism have listed in the forefront of the cause in Great Britain:[1] Maude Dominica Petre (1863–1942). Yet, despite such acknowledgment and despite her own extensive theological writings, Maude Petre has never been the subject of a major critical study.[2]

This study, then, will examine the life and thought of this extraordinary woman who described herself as the "solitary marooned passenger, the sole living representative of what has come to be regarded as the lost cause of Modernism in the Catholic Church."[3] Unlike most other leaders of the Modernist movement, Maude Petre survived the crisis by almost two generations. She not only remained a faithful, though questioning Roman Catholic throughout this period, but because she lived long enough to interact with a considerably changed world, she was able to bring to Modernism itself a critical and creative perspective. It will be necessary, then, to study Maude Petre (or MDP as she often referred to herself in writing) as a religious thinker in her own right, as a friend and supporter of major Modernist figures, and as historian of the movement. In pursuing such an investigation, we follow as well the career of one of the very few women theologians in Catholicism in the first half of this century.[4]

1

But one cannot begin to discuss Modernism—nor Petre's role in it—as if resistance to Roman and papal positions were a startlingly new experience in the English Church. Enthusiasm for the papacy cannot be said to have run riot in Britain during the century of the Reformation. In 1583, for instance, the Venetian ambassador to England reported that "the detestation of the Pope was now so confirmed that no one either of the old [Catholic] nor the new [Protestant] religion could bear to hear him mentioned."[5]

In 1570 Pius V had issued *Regnans in Excelsis*, the papal bull forbidding Catholics' obedience to the "monitions, mandates and laws" of Queen Elizabeth, thus making highly suspect their civil allegiance. In Britain there followed centuries of heavy fines, imprisonments, prohibition of civil rights, and, sometimes, executions for Catholic subjects. Almost two hundred years passed without a fully established Catholic episcopacy.[6]

During the seventeenth century, Catholic ecclesiastical policy was for some time governed by a Chapter of Canons with a decidedly Gallican complexion.[7] Appointments of Vicars-Apostolic by Rome did not succeed in dampening a spirit of independence with regard to certain Roman positions.

In the eighteenth century, one of the principal vehicles of Catholic emancipation was the Catholic Committee (later to become the Cisalpine Club), which came into conflict not only with Roman stances, but also with the decisions of their Vicars-Apostolic. The first president of the Catholic Committee of 1782 was Robert Edward, Lord Petre (1742-1801), great-great-grandfather of Maude Petre. Secretary to the group was Charles Butler. The analysis of E. I. Watkin indicates what the Catholic Committee represented:

> The Committee, Butler in particular, was imbued with Anglo-Gallicanism, nationalist even in religion, disposed to restrict the authority of the Papacy and limit its interference. This however was no novelty devised by the disloyalty, if not schism or heresy, of Butler and his associates, but the expression, indeed the final expression, of an attitude traditional in English Catholicism. . . . What was novel was that Anglo-Gallicanism was not predominantly a layman's attitude. . . . Moreover these men were men of exemplary life and strong faith, devoted to the interests of the Church as they understood them.[8]

Of course, the English Catholics were not unique in their approach at this time; the young American Catholic Church was also giving evidence of a certain measure of independent action.[9]

Maude Petre was intensely aware of the Cisalpine spirit that was part of her national as well as familial legacy. In 1928 she authored *The Ninth Lord Petre*, detailing the works and pronouncements of the Catholic Committee under the presidency of her ancestor. Here one reads the price exacted of eighteenth-century Catholics for their gradual emancipation: oaths, declarations, protestations. A proposed oath of 1789–90 brought the greatest display of Catholic internecine turmoil. The oath itself was based largely on earlier ones professing allegiance to the Protestant succession and declaring it heretical to assert that the pope ought to have civil jurisdiction in the Realm. It further called upon the juror to swear that he acknowledged "no infallibility in the pope."[10]

Although the Vicars-Apostolic had approved of nearly similar oaths in the past, they now balked. In part they disliked the calling of the papal deposing power "heretical and a damnable doctrine," and in part they also disliked the designation "Protesting Catholic Dissenters." The battle lines were soon drawn: the Committee pushing on for the new relief legislation, the Vicars content with the status quo. The members of the Committee, according to MDP, "were prepared to make sacrifices for their faith, but not for any unjust claims of their ecclesiastical ruler."[11] The Committee members did, in fact, have a keen sense not only of the limits of papal power (as they had professed in their oaths) but of episcopal power as well. They wrote to the Vicars: "We have the greatest respect for episcopal authority, and are always disposed to obey its decisions, when applied to proper objects, and confined within proper limitation."[12] During one particularly strong quarrel between the Cisalpine group and the Vicars-Apostolic, one sprightly Cisalpine, Sir John Throckmorton, suggested that clergy and laity should by right choose their own bishops.[13]

But any such right of the laity to choose their bishops was not immediately forthcoming. In fact, the tide was taking quite a different turn: the nineteenth century would be the time not of developing ecclesiastical independence, but of the growth of a thorough Romanism. In the wake of J. Derek Holmes's excellent study *More Roman than Rome: English Catholicism in the Nine-*

teenth Century, it is unnecessary to provide any but the briefest sketch of that period of great change and turmoil in British Catholicism.[14]

If the early part of the century be remembered for the Catholic Emancipation of 1829 and the Oxford movement, the latter part, beginning with the restoration of the national hierarchy in 1850, would be remembered for the ascendancy of ultramontanism. Henry Edward Manning[15] (1808–1892), convert from Anglicanism and later Archbishop of Westminster, was the driving force of the Roman ascendancy. In devotions, in way of life, even in clerical dress, the English must come "into line" with the Roman Church.[16] Along with his lay friend William George Ward (1812–1882), Manning fervently desired a definition of papal infallibility understood in the widest sense: frequent, authoritative papal statements to stem the breakdown of authority and belief in the nineteenth-century world.[17]

When the First Vatican Council of 1869–70 met, Archbishop Manning was perhaps the chief promoter of the definition of papal infallibility.[18] In this he strenuously opposed his fellow countryman Lord Acton (1834–1902), who worked tirelessly for the minority or noninfallibilist side.[19] When the definition failed to be as encompassing as Manning wished, he persisted in his belief by making the domain of papal competence very wide indeed in his pastoral letters to English Catholics.[20]

But the Cisalpine spirit was not totally broken. Maude Petre referred to her own father as "one of the last of the Cisalpines,"[21] and noted in another place that she counted it a special privilege to have been in close contact with this "strong and noble type of Catholicism."[22] MDP would display in her own life a fierce style of independence toward ecclesiastical power, while still according it, in her way, a deep respect. There is surely more than a little resemblance to the spirit and stance of her forebears. It will not, perhaps, be wide of the mark to wonder, as this story unfolds, to what extent this sturdy Englishwoman had drunk deeply from old English Catholic wells. And it will be most pertinent to ask, against such a background and despite a myriad of difficulties, why she clung so tenaciously to the Church of Rome.

1

Victorian Sunset:

MDP'S EARLY YEARS

MAUDE PETRE'S ANCESTRAL LINE had been, to put it gently, diverse. Sir William, an early, knighted Petre (d. 1572), had been an undersecretary of state to the Crown and had been involved in the suppression of monasteries. MDP's withering comment about this progenitor was that "he flourished and grew fat under circumstances that were fatal to men like Sir Thomas More."[1]

The second Lord Petre (d. 1637) attained a small literary notoriety when his marriage was celebrated as the subject of Edmund Spenser's *Prothalamion*. Robert, seventh Lord Petre (d. 1713) was the "adventurous baron" of Alexander Pope's *Rape of the Lock* who made off with a lock of Belinda's hair. The ninth Lord Petre (d. 1801) was not only a leader of the Catholic Committee, but also a Grand Master of the English Freemasons.

It was into a family of such minor renown that Maude Dominica Mary Petre was born on August 4, 1863, at the family estate, Coptfold Hall, close to the village of Margaretting in Essex. Dominica was chosen as the infant's middle name because she was born on the feast of St. Dominic. The mother, Lady Catherine Howard, daughter of the Earl of Wicklow, had been a convert to the Catholic faith.

On the morning of Maude's birth, Lady Catherine had been in attendance at Mass at 8:30 and was reading a French novel at 11 a.m. Between these two events, Maude Dominica entered the world. She would later consider it symbolic that her mother delivered between two such activities, representing her daughter's mixed tendencies to religion and paganism.[2]

Maude's father, Arthur, was a younger son of the thirteenth

Lord Petre. Arthur arranged for his ten children to receive a careful Catholic education in the home. His daughter doubted if the Cisalpine father ever wholly accepted the doctrine of papal infallibility. Such reluctance she considered in part due to an old suspicion among the English that the doctrine had tendencies that were as political as they were religious.[3]

The remembrances of the child growing up in this man's house were of austerity and boredom, though neither was unrelieved. The children, as MDP herself was willing to admit, managed in their own way to have a riotous good time. There was overall a pervasive sense of religious destiny and of the claims of the Catholic faith:

> As to the Church, there was no question about it. She contained for us all that we needed. We were inside, totally inside, without the least notion of there being any rightfully habitable place outside. . . . She contained us, held us, embraced us; she fulfilled all our spiritual needs, had the answer to all our spiritual questions.[4]

It was within this atmosphere of faith that the young Maude Petre settled upon a threefold ambition: to become a saint, a philosopher, and a martyr. She chose as her patron St. Catherine of Alexandria, a representative of this triple ideal.[5]

About her tenth year, Maude began to experience that once frequent scourge of adolescent spirituality—scrupulosity. For about three years the affliction persisted, complete with terrors of sudden death and eternal damnation. At last a Jesuit confessor forbade all examination of conscience and the least mental reference to sin in any form for one year. The prescription worked, and in later years the patient was able to counsel and aid others who suffered the same malady.[6]

Around the year 1880, when she was seventeen, Maude fell very much in love and probably would have married "had there been more than a passing attraction on the other side." But as MDP herself admitted: "I was overwhelmingly shy. . . . We had not been taught to bring our goods to market, and I had a crushing sense of propriety." And with a quite non-Victorian candor, she also later acknowledged:

> I was rather over- than under-sexed; and I think that, had I with the temperament of my early years, been born into the social

freedom of the present day, I might have had some rather startling love affairs, unless religious motives prevailed where convention had abdicated.[7]

Before she was twenty, Maude Petre had suffered the loss of both father and mother, who died within two months of one another. Her mother's death entailed responsibilities for the young Maude which precluded, as she judged it, further marital possibilities. Looking back, more than half a century later, she acknowledged that matrimony would have given her an "anchorage in life." Overall, though, she concluded that she was "glad to have lived my own life and shared the life of others in a measure which I could not have done as a married woman."[8]

By the mid-1880s, when she had attained young adulthood, Maude was experiencing yet another kind of spiritual trauma—religious doubt. And this was to be but the beginning of an ongoing, torturing phenomenon in this Englishwoman's life: "I think few souls, religiously disposed, can have been more persistently tormented with doubts than myself."[9]

Of course religious doubt was no stranger to sensitive spirits in the era of the Victorian sunset, the last years of the nineteenth century. Tennyson, Carlyle, Matthew Arnold, and countless others had begun "to falter where they firmly trod" before. Advancing technologies, Darwinism, biblical criticism, the study of Oriental religions, and nascent psychological researches—all made the later Victorian years a time of profound questioning, and in a way set some of the agenda for the Modernist movement.

What were the more specific triggers for Maude Petre's doubts? She traced out twin sources:

> My scepticism results from the twofold sense of the immensity of the universe, physical or metaphysical, and the inadequacy of the human mind. Why do I doubt—or feel disposed to doubt? Simply because the whole business is so tremendous that we cannot possibly get to the bottom of it.[10]

And she was able to assign those very stimuli that intensified doubt at differing periods of her life:

> Science staggered me when I was young—history when I was middle-aged—and now it is the prevailing sociological conception of a humanity sufficient to itself. It seems to me that during my

lifetime, I have been the witness of three distinct waves of doubt and disbelief that have swept the world.[11]

In her youth, she considered, the intellectual world was suggesting increasingly that "ultimate causes were at a discount."[12]

And where could she turn in such difficulty? Miss Petre sought out that very Jesuit confessor who had been her strength during her bout with scrupulosity, most likely Father William Humphrey (1839–1910).[13] He urged her to picture to herself all the holy, wise people of the past who had believed devoutly, and to see her own lone self on the other side. But she immediately saw, of course, that the group of thoughtful doubters was not so much solitary as legion.

Next she sought out yet another Jesuit, Father Peter Gallwey (1820–1906), described by David Schultenover as an ardent devotee of papal power.[14] Gallwey thrust before MDP the definitions of the First Vatican Council:

> If anyone says that the one and true God, our creator and Lord, cannot be known with certainty with the natural light of human reason by means of the things that have been made: let him be anathema.[15]

Accordingly, he assured her it was a mortal sin to deny certain proof. He further insisted that if she studied the thought of St. Thomas Aquinas at Rome, she would be rendered immune from doubt for the rest of her life. Looking back nearly a lifetime later, MDP concluded "it was a fairly crazy idea," but off she went.[16] Her perplexed aunt, Lady Lindsay, told her overly inquisitive friends: "Maude has gone to Rome to study for the priesthood."[17]

Years later, after Tyrrell had gotten to know the formidable Maude Petre, he composed a punning verse called the "Rome Express" to commemorate her pilgrimage for certitude:

> Lo, in the rear an Amazon who shoves
> And murmurs to herself: I feel it moves;
> Herself immobile, nothing can defeat her;
> Rock versus Rock and Petre versus Peter.[18]

Study arrangements in Rome may rightly be termed "Victorian" in style. Miss Petre lodged with a widow lady and engaged a maiden companion to walk with her and be a chaperone during lessons. "It would not have been correct," she noted, "to be visited by an ecclesiastic, day after day."[19]

Just as Schultenover and Ellen Leonard have pointed to a rigidly orthodox phase in George Tyrrell's early development, so is it possible to discern a rigidity in the early Petre.[20] Her early publications in the mid-1880s give no evidence of the inner doubts of the Roman student. An article on Victor Hugo in the *Month* in 1885 berates the French writer for believing too much in human perfectibility and not enough in the victory of grace. "One by one," MDP wrote, ". . . he cast off the graces of his baptism."[21]

Likewise, an article on Carlyle in the autumn of the same year took Carlyle to task for individuality and Emerson for subjectivity. MDP referred to the current intellectual climate as a "fashionable intellectual fog" and a "haze of conjecture."[22]

Apparently by the late 1880s and early 1890s Maude was finding some measure of personal religious stability. On March 13, 1890, she entered the novitiate in London of the Society of the Daughters of the Heart of Mary.[23]

This religious community, founded in France in 1790, continues in existence today throughout the world. The Society seeks to foster in its members through religious vows "a life that is at the same time both contemplative and active." Members do not necessarily live together in religious community; nor do they necessarily wear distinctive religious dress. Evidencing themselves as a group founded during the French Revolution, members might be living "in the world" with those around them unaware of their professed religious status.[24]

In February 1896 Maude Petre professed five-year vows in the Society and shortly thereafter was selected first a local and then a provincial superior of the community. Before her severance with the Society in 1907, MDP showed herself a most zealous member by promoting orphanages and settlement houses among the poor, and also by instruction of converts.[25]

Entry into administrative work may often mean the sharp curtailment of research, writing, and personal activities; this was not the case with Maude Petre. In 1898 she contributed 1,000 pounds to the construction of Westminster Cathedral.[26] Her writing not only continued; it increased. Her first full-length book had appeared in 1896, *Aethiopum Servus: A Study in Christian*

Altruism, a life of Peter Claver. Articles written near the century's end, such as "Stray Thoughts on the Woman's International Congress" and "Shades of the Prison House," begin to show more of an openness to the modern experience. Her approach never loses a critical bite, however, as she wars on the "monotonous and barren" materialism of the age.[27]

Careful evaluation of the Petre writings in this period reveals new influences and insights at work. In fact, the years 1898–1900 represented a critical turning point for MDP. They are the years in which a steady correspondence began with such figures as George Tyrrell,[28] Henri Bremond,[29] and Friedrich von Hügel.[30]

In 1900, Petre also formed an enduring literary friendship with the writings of Juliana of Norwich, the fourteenth-century mystic. Especially in Juliana's doctrine that God "would make all well that was not well," she saw a kind of solution to the problem of the eternity of hell that had not ceased to plague her since childhood.[31] Significantly enough, Tyrrell's controversies had begun with an article on hell entitled "A Perverted Devotion," published in the *Weekly Register* in 1899.[32]

The year 1900 also brought with it unprecedented fatigue, depression, and mental distress to Maude Petre. It was at this time that Tyrrell wrote her a letter of encouragement that is a masterpiece of English understatement:

> I feel very convinced that you will soon collapse altogether. . . .
> Your hair is crowded with a hopeless tangle of concern which you
> have no leisure to comb and arrange and so the tangle gets more
> distressing every day.
>
> I don't think it is quite wholesome that you as yet wish to die,
> though I fear I know the sort of desperate perplexity from which
> the wish springs. . . . What you need more than death is leisure
> to space out your crowded experiences and to digest and profit by
> them.[33]

Tyrrell further suggested the advisability of resigning the superiorship and the keeping of a diary. MDP was to wait four years before acting on the former suggestion, but the latter she acted on at once, beginning a diary in September 1900.[34]

These diaries are most valuable sources, especially in the early years of turbulence of the Modernist movement before the fullness of the storm broke in 1907. Within these eight hand-written journals are to be found not only the intellectual turmoil of a theological movement, but the personal torment of a great-hearted and deeply spiritual woman as well.

2

New Century—New Influences

IN HER DIARIES, Maude Petre was to look back on her participation in a retreat given by George Tyrrell in July 1900 as the "beginning of a new life"[1] for herself. Nor was this the mere rhetoric of an enthusiastic retreatant. As late as 1937 she recorded, "My acquaintance with George Tyrrell changed the course of my life and affects it even now. . . . from the hour in which George Tyrrell entered my life something happened for good."[2] It was because of Tyrrell, MDP wrote, that she was able to shed aloofness, excessive reserve, and dogmatic rigidity.[3]

Nor was Maude Petre any less specific in enumerating those factors she thought herself to have brought to Tyrrell's growth. She sought "to share his dangers, to check his imprudence and to ensure his perseverance." Without her own "often irritating" presence, she felt, "he might have been drawn into groups unworthy of his sympathy and cooperation."[4]

Tyrrell, for his own part, gave evidence of the way in which his friend was able to "serve some purpose" in his life. He wrote to Maude Petre in a letter of December 1900 discussing his disagreements with the Jesuits and concluded:

> I tell you all this because your heart is mine, and I want at least one confessor in whom I can trust. You just prevent me turning into stone, and then when I think how inaccessible you must always be, I feel harder than ever and put you out of my mind lest you should weaken my ruthlessness to no purpose.[5]

After Tyrrell's death, when Maude Petre was criticized for her posthumous publication of some of his writings, she commented, "I did not begin to build without counting the cost."[6] The cost of her companionship over the years was considerable. In her

1937 autobiography she tells of the advice sent her by the famous spiritual advisor Abbé Henri Huvelin about her relationship with Tyrrell: "Tell her that it is God who sends her to this soul – she will have much to suffer." She added: "The latter part of the prophecy was true enough."[7]

The diaries for the early part of the Petre-Tyrrell friendship reveal a deeply troubled woman. They show Maude Petre as emotionally attached to Tyrrell, but "determined to make this affection all that it ought to be; to constantly raise it and purify it – otherwise it is not only displeasing to God, but insulting to its object."[8]

Ever a frank person, Maude Petre wrote Tyrrell in an attempt to explain her own affection, and later published Tyrrell's response in its entirety in her autobiography. (Her own letter to him is not extant.) Tyrrell spoke in his letter of the need never to deviate from the highest standards of what a relationship such as their own should be. He indicated doubt that he was any longer capable of a very "ardent or absorbing" attachment. Other women, Tyrrell said, had cared for him, but on a total misunderstanding of him; "it was as though a letter intended for someone else had been delivered to me." He went on to reject any love that was not critical and intelligent, or that resulted in a clinging attachment.[9] And in December 1900, he closed a letter to MDP with the phrase: "Yours, I know not how. G.T."[10]

But of Maude Petre's affection for George Tyrrell there can be little doubt. In her autobiography she wrote:

> It was between thirty and forty . . . that I knew, in the complete sense, what it was to love. . . . I had that consciousness of eternity; that sense that nothing else mattered on earth or in heaven; that it was the one priceless pearl for which all else could be sold or cast away as dross . . . that I could accept slavery or ill-treatment; that, finally, as I said to the one friend who guided me through this experience, I would "go to hell with him" if that was where he went.[11]

The diary entries throughout these middle years of Maude's life, especially in the autumn of 1900, leave no doubt whatsoever that it was of Tyrrell she wrote, and it was the French cleric Henri Bremond, "the one friend who guided me," in whom she confided her innermost thoughts and feelings about Father Tyrrell. Those feelings, ambivalent though they may have been, MDP eventually specified in her own mind after the most wrenching of struggles. As a result of these scrutinies she chose to make a perpetual vow of celibacy in May 1901. From that time on, she dedicated herself mightily to the cause of preserving Tyrrell's priesthood.

"To me," Maude Petre would say, "the continuance of his life as a Catholic priest mattered more than anything else, and I would certainly have died to secure his spiritual safety."[12] The Petre Diary of All Saints Day, November 1, 1900 recorded:

> I fall into agonies of fear for him. How will it end? O may God give him peace and strength; how willingly I would sacrifice mine for him. I have not much to sacrifice now – life is so painful, so anxious, so weary . . . that awful abyss of doubt that yawns on every side.[13]

Maude Petre was not compelled to give her life in her special quest, but, as she herself suggested, she knew a full measure of suffering. The friendship that was "as pure on both sides, and as disinterested in its common aims as any friendship could be"[14] was sometimes quarrelsome as well, even controversial.[15]

The controversial nature of the friendship is noted by Petre herself in the autobiography. She and Tyrrell were both living in Richmond, Yorshire between 1902 and 1904; Maude was looking after two young nephews whose parents were in China. The rather special nature of her religious community allowed such a guardianship. But there was criticism of her frequent companionship with Tyrrell and "very reluctantly," she was induced to leave Richmond.[16]

It was perhaps inevitable that such a special type of friendship should be misunderstood. The comments that the principals of the relationship left behind them on the situation are the terse kind that can sometimes say more than volumes. When Tyrrell was considering moving to Storrington in 1906, he wrote his friend Baron Friedrich von Hügel, "Enough that there is nothing to hide."[17] And Maude, for her part, confided to her diary: "It simply comes to this that one has to bear the gossip and the loneliness and the sense of failure besides."[18]

About the same time that Maude Petre was coming to her

friendship with Tyrrell, there also appeared the beginning of a considerable correspondence between herself and Baron Friedrich von Hügel (1852-1925).[19] The Baron had been a family friend of the Petres, and Maude's first remembrances of him are from her girlhood. As a young woman, she remembers seeing him fairly often; but, she says, "I was then in my rigidly orthodox phase: he thought me stiff and hidebound, which I certainly was."[20] It was after Maude began reading St. Teresa of Avila and "entered on a wider spiritual horizon" that she and the Baron became close friends.[21]

The Baron provided bibliographies and encouraged his friend to wider reading. It gave him great pleasure that Rudolf Eucken's works, especially *Der Kampf um einen geistigen Lebensanhalt*, which he had presented her as a gift, were impressing Maude. In her autobiography MDP declared von Hügel's friendship to be a "golden gift." In the first stages of the Modernist crisis, she was to remember him as "undoubtedly our leader," but admitted that the Baron did not keep his "hold" on many of them to the end.[22]

Although Maude Petre tended to extol the intelligence, insight and spirit of von Hügel, she shied away from his leadership. He was, she thought, too prudent and too cautious in his approach to authority. She wrote:

> I think some thought that he had no right to be safely on board when so many of his friends were in the water. Even if they stepped over when he had advised them not to do so, it may have been that it was time for him to step over also.[23]

At the turn of the century, in addition to Tyrrell and von Hügel, Maude Petre also befriended the French Jesuit Henri Bremond (1865-1932), a minor actor in the Modernist drama that was to follow.[24] In the early 1900s she had turned to Bremond as a confessor and had found a spiritual strength through him. Maude would exercise a reciprocal influence on her French friend. Bremond was deeply troubled in those years, anxious to leave the Society of Jesus, but fearing the upset that his departure would cause his family, especially his two Jesuit brothers. He considered the secular priesthood as an alternative to Jesuit life and also the lay state. Apparently here too MDP was trying to work her restraining influence. Bremond wrote her: "Of course I am and always will be able of many foolish things, but whatever I may do, you must say to yourself that, for you, I could have done much more."[25] And later he wrote, "I want you to be my good genius to the end. . . . No one has loved me or will love me as you do."[26] Eventually Bremond left the Jesuits to become a secular priest.

Tyrrell, von Hügel, Bremond – these men will all appear again in these pages. It has been necessary here to introduce them as part of the *dramatis personae*. Maude Petre, after all, tended to see her own involvement in the Modernist movement largely in terms of these individuals:

> My chief share in the Modernist movement was through my friendship with three men . . . von Hügel, Henri Bremond, George Tyrrell. I would label these friendships as close, closer, closest. . . . I bestirred myself at times, and struck my oar into the waters; but I was more concerned with the thoughts and actions of others than with my own.[27]

But in 1900, the year that these friendships were blossoming, the oar had not yet struck the water; the Modernist waters, in fact, were not yet to the full, much less to the flood. Maude Petre, having produced one book, *Aethiopum Servus* (1896), continued to write short articles for the *Month* and began to contribute material to the short-lived *Weekly Register* and *Monthly Register*.

The *Month* for February 1901 carried her review-article "An Englishwoman's Love Letters," based on a book of the same name by Laurence Housman. The novel had been one of the sentimental sensations of the year for late Victorian London. Maude, finding the story of unrequited love "beautiful beyond words – except those of the book itself," felt compelled to comment on such love in the article.[28]

Some critics had found this story of an exclusive type of love to be pagan in its style; not Maude Petre. There might be some element of truth in the charge, she admitted. But MDP also maintained that deeped-seated love could also open the human soul to "more faith and religion than it had ever known."[29] Moderns do not fully realize, she maintained, that "it is in our relationships to man that we find the best guidance to our relationship with God and vice versa."[30]

One human being's love for another, she thought, as it grows ever deeper, "begins to seek God, for it has laid hold of what, in man, is most hidden, and also most divine." Such an intense human love penetrates beyond the visual, the tactile, even the intellectual to some "deeper unending reality" which roots personality.[31] And because mystery, which is the unknowable, is thus at the heart of love, a sense of fear and loneliness must of necessity be involved.[32]

This early essay traces out a fundamental theme that will run like a thread through many of Maude Petre's later writings: the incarnational truth that human thought and experience are the primary locus of spiritual realities. As will be evident from the investigation of Petre's writings, her conception of God's immanence in man is very far from excluding transcendence. One might find a very close parallel to her thought in that of Maurice Blondel (1861–1949) that French philosopher who so deeply influenced Modernist thinkers and yet whose own work never fell under official condemnation. In fact, George Tyrrell, reading Blondel's *L'Action* in August 1900, wrote to Maude: "He is only saying elaborately and technically what we both know in a simpler form."[33] And one of Blondel's central contentions was that transcendent Being is immanent in human experience, but that that which is *within* us is not of us.[34] It will, at any rate, be of interest to watch this theme, for the cry of total immanence will be one of the charges leveled against Modernism in 1907.[35]

November 1901 found Maude Petre approaching the question of God's presence in the world from a different perspective. In a three-part series entitled "Devotion and Devotions" in the *Weekly Register*,[36] she raised the problems of providence and determinism. One measures the worth of special devotions, she had begun, not by any mere appeal to antiquity; rather, one asks if the devotion is truly *living*, springing from "the soil of our spiritual life."[37]

So often, devotions are reduced to nothing more than prayer for specific objects or favors; piety becomes a kind of shield against those "outrageous slings and arrows" of fate. The British lady who had gone to Rome to study St. Thomas in the 1880s now turned to the same Angelic Doctor to argue for her own wider perception of devotional life.

Drawing on the wisdom of St. Thomas, MDP wrote that those devotions are most spiritually productive that draw creatures to God and not just to the temporal favors the Deity might grant. On the practical level, the prayer and life-style of Jesus obviously invite Christians to approach God for material as well as spiritual needs. But push this to an extreme, she warned, and one has God at work changing the weather, finding keys, helping people to catch trains. Isn't the faith higher, she asked, that looks not for these things, but for that reward Aquinas sought – "only thyself, Lord"?[38]

During the year that "Devotion and Devotions" was written, Maude Petre had been reading widely and recording authors and titles in her diaries. She had read, for example, Bremond's *L'Inquietude Religieuse* and commented to her journal that Pusey, Newman's friend, had stayed out of the Church for the same reason he would have remained within it had he converted; he failed to make his life an ongoing questioning experience once his mind and affections were set. Tellingly, Maude Petre wondered, "can we condemn in Catholics the very temper of mind we encourage in Protestants?"[39] Thus was she showing evidence of the high value she placed upon questioning within the Church.

Even a partial listing of Maude Petre's readings between 1901 and 1903 reveals her own wide interests in various religious approaches: Henri Bergson, Thomas Hardy, Coventry Patmore, Alfred Loisy (*La Religion d'Israel*),[40] Rudolf Eucken, William James, Edward Caird, Cardinal Newman (*The Essay on Development*), John Stuart Mill, the Quirinus Letters of Ignaz Döllinger, and studies of Buddhism which she pursued with George Tyrrell.[41]

Even further evidence of MDP's insistence on the necessity of intensive questioning within the Church appeared in an article published in January 1902. The real enemies of spiritual truth, she wrote, are those "who repress the endeavor to renew it in each age of the world." Life is, after all, "a continued renewal, and mere repetition is another name for the decay that leads to death." The genuine lovers of tradition, on the other hand, "are not those who guard it from the last breath of criticism, but those who search and sift it, who distinguish in it that which is temporary and passing from that which is lasting and eternal."[42] The sentiment clearly reflects the developmental thought of a Newman, and anticipates in some manner John XXIII's landmark "Message to Humanity" at the opening of the Second Vatican Council on October 11, 1962.

In another article written in 1902, MDP turned from the somewhat abstract question of doctrinal development to a very practical question of the role of the priest in society. "The Order of Melchisidek" examined briefly the phenomenon of anti-clericalism and indicated that many who consider themselves the strongest critics of the priesthood are actually heavily tinged with clericalism. The paradox is only apparent, however, and is readily explained: many are severe critics precisely because they demand much of the priest that it is not his duty to supply; thus they show themselves much too dependent on their priests in the first place.[43]

British believers of her time were scandalized and souls "unhinged," Maude Petre wrote, by some clerical scandal or display of ignorance, but this certainly was not the case with their old English Catholic ancestors. These ancestors had deep reverence for a priest as administrator of the sacraments, but did not turn to him for guidance or spiritual direction. "Within a certain province, those earlier Catholics paid the priest the sincerest respect, but this province was very strictly circumscribed and limited."[44] In the thick of the Modernist battle, Maude Petre, truly an old Catholic daughter, would show a similar regard for limitation in the Church's guardianship.

Attitudes had changed in England due to the Romanizing influence of many converts, and Maude Petre conceded that the old English Catholics may not have had an ideal spiritual approach. But, she maintained, one must still guard the limits carefully. Obviously priests should be enlightened and have a good measure of education; the issue is rather whether they are to be accredited with supremacy of mind in Catholic thought. Hard as a sincere priest may try to keep abreast of the many new problems rising in both Church and world he may still be intellectually inferior to those who seek out his advice. The strength the priest offers, then, will be a spiritual one, and its source will not be in learning alone. Accordingly, "it is only the more ignorant classes . . . that can continue to look to their priests for a final solution of an intellectual difficulty, even in the religious order."[45]

But the solution for the educated Catholic is not to avoid the spiritual counsel of the priest, nor to turn to an educated layman as spiritual guide. Although the priest may not possess the final answer to a theological problem, he does possess a special power of guidance, if he lives up to the full demands of his priestly office. That power comes from the special mission that is his: "to help in the shaping of passing events to temporal ends," of living his priestly responsibility of being the "representative, in a special manner of the unchanging cause of God in a changeable world."[46]

Maude Petre's conception of the role of the priest found a parallel in her view of the Church's role in the world. In "Unum Necessarium," published in the *Monthly Register*, she had asked the question of the relationship of "the Church in the Modern World." And like the conciliar document of similar title some sixty years later, she held that the Church deals with modernity not by appropriating the material elements of the world to herself and then turning them toward the spiritual. Rather, the Church must enter into and appropriate the *world's* eternal and spiritual elements. The task of the total Church remains that which her priests act out in a special way – pointing to the unchanging cause of God in a changeable world.

The Church has not only to instruct, challenge, and lead the world to a proper spiritual perspective; the Church must open herself to positive influences from the world itself:

> What is truly essential is that the Church should know how to receive and absorb and direct that swelling tide of thought and action which raises creation to God as she, in a sense, brings God to creation. Her part in life, like that of her children, is rather directive than creative. . . . The Church is distinguished from the world by her final principle and test and standard to which all the rest is referred, but her spiritual life will be fuller in proportion as she absorbs more of the wealth of nature and all mankind.[47]

This represents an ideal toward which the Church may strive. In the historical order, though, the Church sometimes gives evidence of misdirection and failure. In an unsigned article in the *Weekly Register* entitled "Alma Mater," Petre asked why the members of the Church persist in assertions about the glories of the Church to an unbelieving world. Not satisfied to proclaim their faith in her spiritual destiny, such overly zealous Catholics try to prove that the Church wants also to proclaim a worldly trium- phalism. Is it not possible to speak humbly of the Church, MDP asked, and still be loyal to her as Alma Mater?

Yes, such loyalty is possible, for the Church has reason for both pride and humility. "She is glorious by reason of the seed which she bears within her; she is lowly by reason of the imper- fection of her own response." Just as modern psychology has re- vealed inner depths and unconscious levels in all men, Maude wrote, so does the Church have its own hidden inner resources. "The spiritually rich and noble and powerful are hidden within her, working out her destiny as the seed works in the dark, damp ground." Such forces may only be drawn forth from time to time by the "Hand of God, the great Mesmerist" in periods of crisis. And yet members of the Church continue to boast of that which *has* been done "instead of resting our hopes on that still hidden glory which is yet to be revealed." We fail to recognize "with Christ Himself, the smallness of that seed which He cast into the earth and committed to the seething mass of human possibilities."[48]

Throughout 1901 and 1902, then, MDP began to stake out a special theological territory for herself: the Church and its rela- tionship to modern culture. Her ecclesiology roamed freely over questions of asceticism, discipline, mission, and reform. Such writ- ings anticipated the call of the Second Vatican Council for a church *semper reformanda*—always in need of reform. They also demanded of that same church an intense, ongoing questioning, that which a later generation would call "dialogue with the secular world."

"Church" for Maude Petre was that force in history that pointed men and women toward the truly humane and the deeply spiritual both in themselves and in the world-at-large. Each in- dividual without exception is possessed of a reality beyond mere seeming, a "hidden wholeness" as Thomas Merton would later style it. The Church, Maude Petre held, was the reality most highly suited to bring that which was hidden into the redeeming light of day.

In the years immediately before the onset of the Modernist difficulties, Petre had found a theological port for the brewing storm. The three books she published during the Modernist years—*Where Saints Have Trod* (1903), *The Soul's Orbit* (1904), and *Catholicism and Independence* (1907)—all would show the influence of the central role that the doctrine of the Church held in the thought of Maude Petre.

3
Emerging Conflicts, 1903–1907

THE YEAR 1903 WAS to prove in many ways momentous for the rapidly developing Modernist movement. A storm already was raging over Abbé Alfred Loisy's 1902 *L'Evangile et L'Eglise*, a reply to Adolf Harnack's *Das Wesen des Christentums*, when the Abbé produced the inflammatory sequel, *Autour d'un petit livre*, in 1903.[1] In replying to the Protestant liberalism of Harnack, Loisy had also put forward some of his own critical opinions: the Church and sacraments were not directly instituted by Jesus; Jesus had erred in His expectation of the immediate advent of the Kingdom. In the second of these two "little red books" especially, Loisy had insisted on the autonomy of the historical science in the face of dogmatic assertions.[2]

Meanwhile in England in 1903, George Tyrrell was at work on his *Letter to a University Professor*, at first intended for private publication and circulation. This was published in 1906, as *A Much-Abused Letter* and ultimately led to his final dismissal from the Jesuits.[3] In the *Letter* Tyrrell tried to respond to the felt religious need of intellectuals of his time, suggesting approaches that must have seemed to his critics minimalistic with regard to the visible Church. Tyrrell wrote, for example:

> For as the Roman Communion is not co-extensive with the whole of the spiritual world, with the Invisible Church, so neither is her creed, her collective mind and teaching, co-extensive with the mind of the whole, with that Vision of which Faith is a sharing.[4]

If the thought of Loisy and Tyrrell, symptomatic of some of the new thinking in Roman Catholic circles in the early years of the new century, proved liberating and helpful to some, it was controversial to others. Pope Leo XIII, who had died July 20,

1903, has been considered rather lenient by some about the potentially dangerous new currents of thought. Père Léonce de Grandmaison has written: "In the failing hands of the aged Pontiff, the reins grew a little slack toward the end."[5] Few would be inclined to speak of his successor as having been slack in his reactions to the new thought.

Giuseppe Sarto, having ascended the papal throne as Pius X, on August 4, 1903, soon gave evidence of a stern approach. In the first encyclical of the reign, *E Supremi Apostolatus Cathedra*, the new pope warned that he would "take the utmost care to see that members of the clergy are not ensnared by the cunning of a certain new science which is endeavoring to pave the way for rationalism."[6] The encyclical was dated October 4, 1903; on December 4, by a decree of the Holy Office, five of Loisy's books, including *L'Evangile et L'Eglise* had been placed on the Index. In the same decree two works by Abbé Albert Houtin were also condemned, and directives were shortly forthcoming against the laymen Edouard LeRoy and Antonio Fogazzaro.[7]

More specifically, what were those aspects of the new theological approaches that would so deeply trouble the Roman authorities? For a full understanding of the Roman attitude it would be necessary to study in some detail the papal documents *Lamentabili Sane Exitu* of July 3, 1907, a syllabus containing sixty-five condemned propositions, and the previously mentioned encyclical, *Pascendi Dominici Gregis* of September 8, 1907. This last presents an overall systematic approach as at least the implicit foundation of the "Modernists"—a name largely given currency by the encyclical itself. Fortunately, thorough studies of the encyclical and analyses of Modernism in general are plentiful[8] and it will be necessary here only to present a kind of working definition or description of the phenomenon in which Maude Petre would play her part. The extent of MDP's own involvement as well as her role as historian and evaluator of the movement will be examined later in these pages. The activities properly designated Catholic Modernism range throughout the twenty years between 1890 and 1910. The papal condemnation and the imposition of an anti-Modernist oath served as its death warrants.[9]

Modernism can be seen as an attempt at a response to the explosion of knowledge and criticism that confronted the believer as a result of nineteenth-century intellectual and scientific developments. Among these disturbing new features of the age, the most prominent would have been: the critical approach to Scripture, the new world of Freudian analysis and psychology, the evolutionary perspective of Darwin that threw so many of the past securities into question, the systematic study of non-Christian religions, the shifting status of working and minority groups in society, the challenge of Marxism and socialism, and the general secularization of Western culture.

To oversimplify not a little, the Modernists sought to confront such challenges head-on, confident in most cases that truth lay profoundly enough snuggled within the bosom of the Roman tradition that it needed only to be restated, and perhaps partly restructured, in order to stand as a valid place of interpretation and integration of life even in the face of the modern insecurities.

The Roman Curia, with the blessing of Holy Father Pius X, tended to favor only the most moderate revision absolutely necessary (as in Leo XIII's support of the French Republic) in order to speak to the modern world. This communication to the modern world, however, presumed secular error, a wrong-turn, an abandoning of the stabilities of the past; it was grudging and little more than occasionally tolerant.

The Modernists, on the other hand, approached more closely what might be termed enthusiasm in their overtures to new times. Just as subsequent history would show the papal-curial approach to have been overly tight, so would it show many of the Modernists to have been somewhat uncritical in their zeal for the modern spirit. As Karl Rahner and Herbert Vorgrimler expressed it: "Modernism . . . proposed wrong solutions to many problems it had grasped aright."[10]

Roman Catholic Modernism, then, was one of several attempts of Christianity to respond to the modern experience during the crucial century from the Congress of Vienna (1815) to the assassination at Sarajevo (1914). Other attempts had included: on the left, Protestant liberalism, the Social Gospel movement, and the doctrinal development theories of Newman; and on the right, Evangelical fundamentalism within Protestantism and the rigid reassertion of papal authoritarianism in Catholicism.

As its methodological base, Modernism insisted upon the conviction that "the modern mind is entitled to judge what is true or right in accordance with its own experience, regardless of whether or not its conclusions run counter to tradition and custom."[11] There is no evidence that Modernism was highly organized or coordinated in its challenge to many traditional approaches within Roman Catholicism, but there was often a "tone antagonistic to all ecclesiastical authorities."[12]

Those who know Modernism only through the figure of Alfred Loisy often assume that the basic problem with the movement was centered in the biblical crisis alone. But a more comprehensive understanding of Modernism reveals many more troubling issues at stake. As Heaney indicates, the threat of Modernism was even more fundamental than that of biblical criticism; it was, in fact, threefold:

1) . . . denial of the supernatural as an object of certain knowledge (in the totally symbolic, non-objective approach to the content of dogma which is also related to a type of agnosticism in natural theology);

2) an exclusive immanence of the Divine and of revelation ("vital immanence") reducing the Church to a simple, social, civilizing phenomenon;

3) and a total emancipation of scientific research from Church dogma which would allow the continued assertion of faith in dogma, with its contradiction on the historical level (as understood in certain presentations of the "Christ of faith, Christ of history"; "Church of faith, Church as history" distinctions).[13]

And Rahner and Vorgrimler have provided a brief catalogue of the extreme Modernist perspective that can be summarized as follows:

1) Theology is only a matter of feeling.

2) Religion is solely a product of the unconscious.

3) Neither feeling nor the unconscious must be constrained by reason.

4) Revelation is nothing more than awareness of an interior religious need, the bearers of revelation being such merely because they best objectify this need.

5) Dogma is only a symbolic expression of these objectifications; dogma must change with the progress of civilization.

6) There is a natural need to communicate one's own objectification of religion to others and when this is done, the Church occurs.[14]

And though, of course, not all involved in the movement pushed
to the extremes suggested above, this catalogue of tendencies at
the very least suggests the possibilities of excess, the perimeters to
be avoided by those who were concerned with remaining on the
ground of Christian tradition. It would be a separate judgment in
the case of each Modernist whether and to what extent his or her
own theology crossed critical lines. And the location of the lines
themselves might be understood quite differently in the post-
conciliar Church than in 1907. At any rate, this short summary
may provide the useful background against which Maude Petre
and some of her friends may stand out more clearly in the
development of this study.

For all the theological complexity and sophistication of
the Modernists, it was not to theology as such, but to spirituality that Maude Petre turned in the critical year of 1903 in
her book *Where Saints Have Trod*. As usual, ecclesiology and
spirituality were to be her dominant concern during the Modernist years. *Where Saints Have Trod* was the first of those three
books she produced during the height of the Modernist years,
and one of her first writings to elicit an angry response. In a
review in the *Dublin Review* in October 1904, an anonymous
writer[15] commented that the book should have been subjected to
Church censorship before publication. He judged Maude Petre
fairly harshly:

> Miss Petre seems to be a lady of somewhat advanced views. She
> has got hold of the word "sub-conscious", and uses it to state a
> theory of prayer which has no support either in theology or in
> psychology.[16]

The reviewer criticized the constant use of the word "living"
throughout MDP's work, said it showed the influence of Ritschl,
and further suggested that for Maude, "living" is equivalent to
"adapted to my subjective persuasions." He followed this charge
with an immediate chiding judgment: "Miss Petre is too sound a
Catholic not to recognize that devotion and faith depend on external and objective teaching."[17] And he concluded that she should
never have been encouraged to publish "a series of essays full of
half-truths and crude philosophy, intended for the Catholic Truth
Society."[18] A review in the *Catholic World*, on the other hand,
praised the book for "its abundant evidence of a study of St.

Thomas Aquinas and a wide reading of the classical ascetical writers."[19] What kind of book had occasioned such a varied reception?

Maude Petre's prologue indicated clearly enough her intention of subjecting old devotions and asceticisms to severe questioning with the hope of discovering new depths and meanings within. To describe the old intellectual and spiritual system she employed the image of Ezekiel's valley of bones:

> In each successive age men find themselves standing on a field covered with the bones of those institutions and habits and opinions that have gone before, and again and again, on every fresh occasion, the old controversy arises as to what is to be done with the aforesaid bones.[20]

Some, she said, would think the bones should remain there just as they are, having a prior right to be there; others would insist that they were better buried and forgotten. But the genuine prophet would speak the word of life, and obeying the creative power, the bones would rise up and "claim the privilege not to cumber the earth but to cultivate it."[21] And so the innermost values of the past lived and vivified others through the creative force exercised by the present on the past: "the past cannot speak except through the mouth of the present."[22] Insofar as the old doctrines are possessed of truth, "that truth is eternal and capable of being adapted to the newer knowledge of the present."[23] And in a phrase reminiscent of Harnack, Petre wrote that "we have then to penetrate to the kernel, stripping from it any husks formed by long usage and routine."[24]

Accordingly, the first essay "Commandments and Counsels" probed the value of the religious vocation: how does one contrast the call of the religious life with the demands made on all Christians? Religious all too often glory in some supposed prestige, in that which separates them from others, Petre wrote. They hunger too eagerly for rest and completion, forgetting that "nothing spiritual is unchangeable, and that any life is called a state rather by reason of what it excludes than of what it contains."[25] Thus, the more human side of religious life does demand a "general proficiency in the more rigid obligations of the Christian life."[26] But this no more defines religious life than a mere observance of marriage vows defines the true depth of marriage. And so, if one looks

to the divine or eternal side of religious life, it becomes possible
to say:

> It is but a more intense embodiment of the aspirations common
> to every soul striving towards God through Christ, and, thus
> regarded, all its regulations, however sacred, are but an effort to
> accomplish more completely that which is the will of God for
> every one of us.[27]

Thus does Maude Petre go about stripping the husk of exclusivity
and privilege that had in some cases built up around the inner core
of religious life.[28]

Other traditional ascetical principles are called into scrutiny
as well. One old style of holiness, for instance, suggests that the
holy person should "care nothing for the opinions of men—to
prefer contempt to honor, misunderstanding to appreciation."[29]
Such an approach is laden with contradiction, MDP acknowledged; for example, it demands that the holy ones edify others at
the same time that they should hate their own reputations. Yet
this traditional approach had been widely encouraged in spirituality.[30] Has it now no value?

On the immediate surface, it might seem that the old spirituality has no value, since reputation is "based on an instinct
almost as strong as that of self-preservation itself."[31] And Maude
Petre herself demanded to know by what right a religious practice
can "fly in the face of a fundamental law of our being?"[32] She
found, however, that asceticism is based on a keen insight of the
demands made on people if they are to grow more perfect. She
conceived the purpose of the traditional asceticism to be to call
men and women to "a true reverence for the autonomy of other
minds."[33] That is, people must not be so concerned with imposing
their image upon others as with letting others in their autonomy
and freedom judge and challenge one another to be more than
they already are.[34]

Maude Petre spent other chapters in discussing and reinter-
preting other accepted spiritual axioms that moderns might be
hard put to grasp: that, in a world of constant life and motion,
the spiritual ideal is that of rest; that those who attend only to the
things of earth will find only surfeit and boredom for their efforts.
The working assumption seems to have been that one struggled
to move from bad to good and having become good, found rest.

But, "are we so sure that it is less disturbing to move from good to better than from bad to good?"[35]

In refuting such a position, Petre used words that readers of a later generation might compare with those of Teilhard de Chardin, whom MDP would come to know some thirty years later:

> If first we cared for the world too much, so now there is danger that we may care for it too little. Now it is that we must pass forward to the more complete synthesis, in which we find that God alone is truly good and beautiful, but that His beauty and His glory are to be found in the meanest thing that blows, and that, from a certain point of view, our love for no creature can be excessive. Having thus reached faith in God through our faith in man, we come back to have faith in man through our faith in God.[36]

But the reexamination that was to occasion the most criticism from the *Dublin Review* was in the chapter entitled "Self-Will and Freedom." The burden of the chapter was this: how could the vow of religious obedience be considered a positive value in a world that so highly prized freedom? One must look, MDP said, to the special advantage obedience can bring; it can lead to the eradication of self-will, and "the widening of personal existence by the realization of a larger, fuller life in God." And, further, "the right end of religious obedience is to teach us the true method of self-direction."[37]

For one reading this book after the turmoil over *Pascendi*, it is possible to say that a few themes mentioned in the encyclical do in fact make their appearance here in very mitigated ways and balanced out in the wider context. Thus, for example in the words "we are exiled not only from God, but from ourselves, for in truth it is in ourselves that He is to be found,"[38] it might be possible to see a tendency toward immanence; but it might also be possible to see reference to the age-old doctrine of the Indwelling of the Holy Spirit as well. If there is, in fact, an immanentist tendency in Maude Petre, it persists, as indicated in an earlier chapter, along the lines of a Blondel, and finds its counterbalance in the awareness of transcendence.

In 1904, Maude Petre[39] published *The Soul's Orbit*, although she admitted in the prologue that the book was the result of a literary collaboration. What she did not admit in print until 1912, in the *Autobiography and Life of George Tyrrell*, was that it was George Tyrrell with whom she collaborated.

Once again, as in *Where Saints Have Trod*, the orientation is basically toward the devotional aspects of religion, but *The Soul's Orbit* is at once more systematically organized and more prophetic. Thus, the announced purpose of the book is stated:

> Our hope is to present in these pages a few thoughts which will enable all such to bear *the change which is surely coming*, to be *prepared for the storm*, and to have a dwelling ready *before the old one is demolished*. . . . The aim of this work is to prepare such a devotional attitude of mind as will be undisturbed by any intellectual cataclysm, to bring warmth to the heart even before light has reached the mind. . . . [40]

There is something urgent – even ominous – about such an approach. But it is fully in accord with Maude Petre's drive to subject religion to searching reappraisal and with Tyrrell's orientation of seeing devotion as the determinant of theology – *lex orandi, lex credendi*.[41]

Further, the foreboding tone of the published text finds its echoes in Maude Petre's diary. In February 1904, she recorded: "We are in the throes of the Loisy condemnation."[42] By September of the same year, Maude was evidently afraid that her theological stance comprised her effectiveness in her religious community. She explained her intellectual position and asked if her charge should be removed. The answer, for the present, was that she was to keep it.[43]

October found these cryptic words in the diary: "I have accepted the past, prepared for the future. The new wine has burst the old bottles, but the new wine was worth it."[44] A November entry revealed a new situation: an article of MDP's entitled "Let us Die with Her" had been rejected by the *Catholic World*. They were, she said, "afraid" to publish it.[45]

The Soul's Orbit (which Longmans apparently was *not* afraid to publish) was subtitled "Man's Journey to God," and opened with sentiments that would be as congenial to appreciative readers of Blondel as they would be vexing to those who would eventually be appreciative readers of *Pascendi*:

> Our journeying to God is so pre-eminently a matter of action, experiment, life and movement, that it is needful perhaps to consider

what part thought and knowledge and speech have got to play in the process. . . . It is only in our action, as inspiring and permeating our action, that the Spirit is revealed to us; not in conceptions, or formulas, or propositions.[46]

The genuine spirit of the *Spiritual Exercises* of St. Ignatius, in fact, was said to be based on these lines: that "what we think depends on what we feel far more than our feeling depends on our thought."[47] And *The Soul's Orbit* further indicated that Ignatius thought it wise to use the help of external spiritual directors in order that the individual might eventually become more spiritually autonomous himself. In fact, an ideal spiritual director would "allow the Creator to deal with His creature and the creature with its Creator without intermediary."[48] *The Soul's Orbit* then compares this interpretation of Ignatius favorably with the tenor of thought of Father Isaac Hecker, founder of the Paulists. This suggestion is made by Maude Petre and her collaborator only five years after a French edition of Hecker's life had precipitated the "Americanist" controversy, in which some have seen a foreshadowing of the Modernist concern.[49]

Characteristically, one of the chapters of *The Soul's Orbit* that can be ascribed predominately to Maude Petre's authorship deals with the Church and asceticism, and was entitled "Love Not the World." The world, MDP said, is a kind of invisible Church all its own, with doctrines, regulations, and claims to loyalty from its members. The ultimate combat between church and world is to determine whether selflessness or selfishness shall reign.[50] Only in Christ can the right balance be struck:

Christ is the love of God Incarnate, bringing to us, in word and in deed, the twofold commandment of the love of God and the love of man, each comprehending and supposing the true love of self.[51]

In a later chapter, not specifically Petre's, a theme appeared that she had employed in "Alma Mater" in 1902—that is, that the Church is in part defined by her future possibilities. The writer said that the Church's nature "like that of anything that lives and grows is to be found in her ideal and potentiality."[52] In the ideal, Catholicism and humanity come to be coextensive in their range. Multitudes of true Christians are not within the visible

Church, because "the Church is still in the womb of time. . . ."[53]

But if the Church be in part described by that which is yet to come, it must also be aware of that which has gone before. And so, blending together the many factors in the Church's composition, the writers of *The Soul's Orbit* presented a fairly lengthy account of the Church's development:

> She is the result of the multiplication and gradual cohesion into groups, and groupings of groups, and finally into a single organism, of men filled with the spirit of Christ. As she grew in extension she developed within her formless mass that system of bones and sinews and veins and nerves, those organs of collective thought and speech and action, whereby the light and heat and energy scattered though her myriad members might be focussed and concentrated for the advantage of each and all, and whereby the gathered experience of many nations and many centuries might be kept and pondered in one vast heart. It is through her collective spiritual labour that the hidden and inexhaustible potentiality of that buried Grain of Wheat is slowly revealed and brought to human consciousness, that Christ comes to be understood and interpreted, and is enabled to say to us those many things which the past could not bear; to purify our religious conceptions more and more from their childishness and to lead us into all truth. United with her we enter into a universal life, a universal interest; I live, yet not I, not the separate self, but Christ lives in me, the mystical Christ, the millions of redeemed humanity, past, present, and to come, the kingdom of God on earth.[54]

It would seem to be relatively clear in *The Soul's Orbit*, as it had been in Loisy, that Maude Petre did not consider that the institutional Church had begun with the historical Jesus.[55] Rather, a "formless mass" felt the need for developing "organs of collective thought and speech and action." The development was to be seen, however, as the fruit of the Spirit working "along the lines of Nature."[56]

It is far from likely, however, that the author of *Pascendi* could be pleased with this stance. The encyclical had attacked the conception that the Church was a collection of individual believers whose origin was to be found only in the religious conscience.[57] While *The Soul's Orbit* assigned the origin of the institutional Church to what it called the Spirit of Christ, and not to mere human religious consciousness, it was far from speaking in a traditional manner of Jesus' establishment of the Church.

A catalogue might be compiled of other positions in the 1904 text that would sit uneasily with traditional theological approaches. Thus, Jesus' human intellect is said to have served and interpreted the infinite purpose of His union with the Divine nature, although the human intellect of Jesus "could not wholly comprehend" the Divine union.[58] One is said to be able to hear in the Church the voice of God; but this voice is defined as "the collective God-inspired conscience of the elect of humanity."[59] Also, dogma is said to be "an idol if we vainly think to comprise the infinite within its limits."[60]

Predictably, the *Dublin Review* reviewed the book with a good measure of vehemence, calling it "pretentious." The book, the anonymous reviewer noted, was by a Catholic author, but seemed to be: "an attempt to reduce Catholic teaching to the mind's purely subjective view of revealed truth, and Catholic obligation to a strictly subjective sense called 'conscience.'" The reviewer is generally dissatisfied with references to "an unguarded moment of weariness" in Christ's life, and to the conviction of Christ's Lordship being "brought home with a new supernatural vividness to His human consciousness."[61]

A review in the *American Ecclesiastical Review* was more generally favorable but sensed a need for some modification. One is the statement in *The Soul's Orbit* that the "worship-tendency had to struggle through countless imperfect phases in search of fuller self-consciousness, and of an object that would adequately explain it."[62] Another hesitation was expressed about the account of the temptations of Jesus. Jesus, the book had said, was spared those temptations that follow the violation of conscience. But, the review asked, was he not also spared those that "follow fallen nature co-naturally?"[63]

It was late in 1904 that Maude Petre had commented that the new wine had burst the old bottles but that the new wine had been worth it. She was obviously aware of both new perspectives and emerging conflicts in her life. By the end of 1904, then, MDP had begun to encounter severe criticism of her writings. It was also during that same year that she had questioned her role as superior within her religious community. By February 1905[64] she had, in fact, resigned her superiorship, although she held the post of Provincial Councilor until her final departure from the Society.[65]

For all her personal problems, Maude Petre was fairly active in writing articles for journals during 1905. In April she published an essay on Oscar Wilde's *De Profundis*, the last of her writing to appear in the *Month*. She closed this essay with a touch that would be characteristic of her—an attempt to seek out the best in characters generally unpopular. Of Wilde, she wrote, "he was courageous and consistent in a very dark hour, and has left us an example of how a man may make his fate his own."[66] An article on Schopenhauer published in the same month in the *Catholic World* even found redeeming insights in that thinker.[67]

Beginning in 1905 and continuing into the following year, MDP contributed a series of six articles on Friedrich Nietzsche to the *Catholic World*. This series, happily, caused her to specify her own thought on the subject of eschatology, a topic not frequently covered by others in the Modernist movement.

Nietzsche showed a basic misunderstanding of life everlasting, Petre wrote, conceiving it as both too like, and too unlike this present life: too like when he merely expected present joy more intensely; too unlike when he failed to regard the future as "an essential development of the present," and when he persisted in looking at the present life as "not the seed of the future, but simply the coin wherewith it is to be purchased."[68] And showing a keen insight and balance as she treaded her way through the complex territory of eschatology, Maude Petre opposed to Nietzsche's conception of afterlife a more properly Christian attitude:

> But our faith can point to a better immortality than this; one fraught with nobler possibilities for the future, with a higher estimate of the present. As we have seen that Christian self-love finds its justification in a continual participation of infinite love, so also the present life derives its value and its hopes of immortality from an ever active share in that which is eternal. This world is not only a schoolroom, this life is not only a task, but the former is also a manifestation of spiritual realities, and the latter a commencement of everlasting life. Nothing *shall* be but what, in a measure, already *is*: every true thought of the mind, every right feeling of the heart, every sincere act of the will is full of attain-

ment as well as promise; it is a laying hold of what we are to possess more consciously, more perfectly, but not for the first time hereafter. The kingdom of heaven is within us, as well as to come; the future life will be different, not because it is disconnected from the present one, but because it will be the fulfilment of present possibilities, and will make manifest the secrets of our own soul.[69]

The middle years of the first decade of the century brought forth yet another topic that would be crucial for Maude Petre the rest of her life: the nature of religious authority. This theme figured prominently in an article she published in the spring of 1907 in the short-lived Italian journal *Le Rinnovamento* published at Milan.

The center of human life, she wrote, can be found both within and without the human structure. In their drive for life, individuals attempt to forge a unity between their own energies and that which is the source of those energies. Catholicism could be the central place where the truest interpretation and integration of those energies are gathered together. Unfortunately, though, many who might otherwise look to Catholicism are put off by its seeming distance from the realities of modern life and its heavy-handed use of authority.

The past problem had been that the Church tried to assert its predominance through external domination; in fact, MDP insisted, it had a more fundamental basis on which to decry the extremities of individualistic judgment. Catholicism finds individualism too confining for the structure, the corporateness and the destiny of the human. The human mind is finite; yet humanity possesses a sense of the infinite that drives it to shatter the human limits and to reach for a wide, corporate experience.[70]

Thus, it is strength, not weakness, that urges men and women toward religious authority. If one asks, for instance, where to look for the answers to life's ultimate drives and questions, one soon discovers that it is to the Church, toward the spiritual, and not just to the scientific. But the Church in the past had tried to answer problems by its appeal to authority alone without a sufficient feel for the sense of development and growth.

Development must be seen, in fact, as a characteristic of Catholicity. Only then, MDP suggests, will it be possible to look more properly to the Church as "the unifier of life, the fullness of our own proper personality." Petre concluded her review with sentiments very identifiably Newman's: that the peace individuals seek within the Church should not be a peace of mere stability, but one of quest and development. Delay is death and progress is life.[71]

The years 1903 to 1907 had been frantic and trying ones for Maude Dominica Petre, by then a woman in her early forties. She had been busy reading such writers as Harnack ("over-simplified"),[72] Loisy ("occasionally one-sided and not sufficiently large in his admissions"),[73] and Mrs. Wilfred Ward ("clever, but irritating throughout").[74] MDP not only wrote extensively on her favorite themes of ecclesiology, authority, and spirituality, but she also continued as counselor, confidante, and administrator within her religious community—all of this in addition to her extensive visits and correspondence with Bremond, Tyrrell, von Hügel and others in the Modernist orbit.

But 1907 was to be a watershed year in MDP's life. Not only was this to be the year of the Roman condemnation of Modernism; it would also be the year that she published her *Catholicism and Independence.* This volume placed her squarely and publicly within the Modernist camp and just as decidedly *outside* the religious community she had served for over fifteen years. The stage was now set for an extraordinary conflict of one lone lay-woman against the intellectual tradition of the Church of Rome.

4

Catholicism and Independence

ON CHRISTMAS EVE 1907 Maude Petre received a letter from Archbishop Francis Bourne of Westminster urging her to withdraw her book *Catholicism and Independence* from print. She explained to him that this was not possible. Subsequently, though, she did have an audience with the archbishop in which he asked that no second edition of the book be allowed to appear. The only objection Bourne brought forward, by MDP's account of it, was that *Catholicism and Independence* "suggested cases in which the individual conscience might be in conflict with supreme authority." Maude Petre responded that as far as she was concerned there would be no second edition, but that the matter was not entirely hers to control.[1]

On December 14, MDP had noted in the diary that her religious superior had asked her to withdraw *Catholicism and Independence* as well. As a result of her stance on the book the London Council of the Society refused her permission to renew vows. Accordingly, December 1907 marked the termination of Maude Petre's affiliation with her religious order.[2]

What manner of book brought about such decisive consequences? The prologue alone gave evidence of a controversial nature. While admitting the general need for obedience to governments and laws, MDP also noted: "To our own mental and moral conscience all doctrines and laws must make their last appeal."[3] In fact, the study, subtitled *Studies in Spiritual Liberty*, opened with an appeal to ultimate personal judgment (though made within a context of corporate authority) regarding "all doctrines and laws," or, in another terminology, faith and morals.

The opening chapter, "The Temperament of Doubt,"[4] concerned itself with religious doubt. There may be moral guilt, Petre says, in such a condition; but trying to strengthen the doubter by urging acts of faith on him is "like advising him to dance on a broken leg by way of setting it."[5] Besides, because "our mental mechanism is complicated beyond all our psychological knowledge,"[6] it should be little cause for amazement that people cannot always account for changes in their beliefs.

Besides, there is a kind of doubt that is salutary. She quoted from Robert Browning's *Bishop Blougram's Apology* and commented:

> But let us instead of calling the snake "unbelief," name it "mystery," and surely we shall have a temper of mind which will combine loyal adherence to our faith with unswerving attachment to truth. Because we feel the snake we know that we believe, and, because he stirs beneath our touch, we know that our faith has the fullness and possibilities of life, and is not a stereotyped formula.[7]

MDP also brought forward here a theme to which she would return thirty years later in her autobiography in discussing loyalty to the Church. In the human experience of the spiritual world, there is not a perfect clarity of vision, not overpowering light. But, in this "forest primaeval," she said:

> There is light enough for us just to distinguish the outline of the trees, but not so much that we cannot at times take them for ghosts. Still, the light that glimmers through them is the light by which alone we can walk and guide our steps so as not to stumble or fall.[8]

Maude Petre would return time and again to this theme both in her life and in her writings. At the end of her life, in the autobiographical *My Way of Faith*, she would write:

> The Church has lighted my way. Instead of struggle through a wilderness I have had a road—a road to virtue and truth. Only a road—the road to an end, not the end itself—the road to truth, and not the fullness of truth itself.[9]

Not surprisingly, Maude Petre was hardly alone in the later nineteenth-century British world in holding that the Church and the spiritual life could be fair, but not full, light in the midst of the darkness. In an age of advancing intellectual and religious crisis, Tennyson had in 1850 already sensed: "I falter where I firmly trod" in his *In Memoriam*. In 1867 Matthew Arnold had spoken of the "melancholy long withdrawing roar" of Christian faith. Even the young John Henry Newman had begun to speak of the "encircling gloom" as early as 1833.

And in America, the Kentucky-born Bishop John Lancaster Spalding had found it necessary to write:

> We cannot graph the infinite; language cannot express what we know of the Divine Being, and hence there remains a background of darkness, where it is possible to adore or to mock. But religion dispels more mystery than it involves. With it, there is twilight in the world; without it, night. We are in the world to act, not to doubt.[10]

Maude Petre, then, had entered the lists of those trying to come to grips with the shift of perspective of the modern age. And she too, like so many others, would feel the wrath of those who resisted that which was coming to be.

The second of the essays in *Catholicism and Independence*, "Obedience Spiritual and Not Military"[11] took up the question of obedience to religious authority. All too often obedience in the Catholic Church runs along military lines, MDP wrote. The obedient Catholic may have to defend "forts that he knows to be tottering to destruction from underground mines."[12] As a result, genuine reform has often had to come from outside the Church "in the form of attack and persecution."[13]

Reform and criticism, after all, should be conceived as the concerns of all those who love the task of the Church, Maude Petre insisted. Such a judgment, however, was not especially well received in a Church still decidedly post-Tridentine; it was still a Church—especially in Britain—where almost any change was accounted to be vice far more than virtue. Piqued, perhaps, by these facts of life, MDP snapped at her readers:

> Are we then to say that the Church can never be saved except by the wrongful attacks of those without, or the wrongful rebellion of those within? Are we to garner the fruit of reform and liberty and spiritual renovation, and dispatch to hell those who earned them for us? Is all the loss to be on the side of the reformer; all the gain on the side of the reformed?[14]

Reformers of course, must forfeit large measures of their security:

If we want to be *sure*, both in our own judgment and that of others that we are *right*, then let us stay within the recognized landmarks—for outside them our ordinary tests are inadequate. If God calls any man to the task of reform, He will give him the heart that is strong enough to brave loneliness and uncertainty and the terrors of unexplored night and darkness. He will give him strength to lose his own soul, trusting that, in God, he shall find it again. . . . the true reformer must be without hearth or home or city to dwell in—an exile, who belongs still to his own country, because he will never accept of another in its place.[15]

It is incorrect, according to Petre, to insinuate that the reformer has rejected all loyalty to the Church. Rather, that loyalty has been "transmuted."[16] What Maude Petre, in fact, demanded of her reformer was the power of prophetic vision. The reformer must be able to read the signs of the times, to know when the Church should "sacrifice her outer prestige to a higher cause."[17] The prophetic reformer will have enough love and loyalty for the Church to see that "The Church too must die to live, and must die continually to live continually."[18]

Further, this reformer, as a later chapter indicated, must be wary of those in the Church who resist reform by invoking the divine element of its composition. True, rulers may distinguish the divine and human elements in the Church readily enough in theory, she said, but they often do not advert to the distinction in fact. The only check on the authority of ecclesiastical rulers is one that might be self-imposed: "Even a Czar, with his ministers, may be rightly opposed by a Duma; but pope and bishops may never be limited, in the exercise of their authority, by the opposition of the faithful. . . ."[19]

Given such a state of affairs, Maude Petre felt the importance of distinguishing the visible from the invisible Church. Allegiance to the former should be "less pervasive and supreme" than allegiance to the latter.[20] Trust in the invisible Church, "which is the Church in the fullest and truest sense of the word,"[21] and which in this essay seems to be very much parallel to the domain of conscience,[22] can inspire the faithful to challenge the human Church when it overreaches the bounds of its authority. But just as there are excesses in administration, there can be excesses in resistance: one can foretell neither abuses in the Church nor the legitimate grounds and extent of resistance to such abuse. It is clear, however, that selfish inconvenience can never serve as sufficient reason for any such challenge.[23] And "Even according to this higher religion we are not solitary units, supreme units, supreme and independent; we still need a Church, a spiritual community, and owe deference to that authority which has been to us the chief source of light and grace. . . ."[24]

Maude Petre had spoken in her chapter "Obedience Spiritual and Not Military" of the ongoing need of the Church to undergo many purgative deaths in order to rise renewed. She invoked the theme again at the conclusion of this essay. Doubtlessly referring to her earlier distinction of the visible from the invisible Church, she admitted the impossibility of a disembodied soul working effectively in the world, but insisted that more vitality within the soul should make the body "slighter and more manageable."[25] The price of such new vitality would inevitably be discipline, even chastisement.

But even granting that the Church may need to suffer, the serious Christian will still look anxiously for some signs to read that chastisement or resistance are truly in order. And although Maude Petre had already indicated that prediction in such areas could be risky, she attempted to distinguish spheres of authority within the Church whose confusion could cause conflict. The chapter that takes up such a task, "Personal Responsibility and Expert Authority," stands out as the centerpiece of this controversial book and surely accounted for much of its criticism.

There is, Petre said, a special area within which Church leaders have their own competence and can legitimately claim obedience:

> when our spiritual superiors make definite claims on our intellectual or moral civil obedience, they are speaking . . . in virtue of their departmental authority and are to be obeyed within the limits of that department. . . . Directly our religious rulers make an unlimited claim, they are passing from the restricted to the universal sense of religion, and are appealing to the tribunal that is within each soul, and not to the external authority of pope or bishop.[26]

Here is more than ample evidence for Archbishop Bourne's statement to Maude Petre that her book "suggested cases in which the individual conscience might be in conflict with supreme authority." Not only had this material pointed to possible conflicts; it had placed limits within which the institutional Church may work and claim rightful allegiance. Once again, the ultimate appeal of the author is to conscience – though here conscience is explicitly understood in its corporate dimensions.[27] Thus, while Church authority can demand absolute obedience in its own sphere, in ultimate spiritual matters it can only appeal, not command.

One could wish that Maude Petre had helpfully provided a catalogue of what material specifically fell under the aegis of the visible Church; wishing, however, does not make it so, and no such catalogue appeared. She had already allowed that the Church could speak in the name of theology as "defined and limited science," but exactly how this relates to dogma and revelation is left unspecified. Official Church rulers may also speak from time to time, MDP wrote, "in the name of religion in its transcendent and universal sense." They would still be speaking within their area of competence, and yet their commands in such cases, "though far more solemn, are by no means so positive, nor can they be fulfilled in the same literal manner."[28]

When she spoke of "solemn" utterances on the part of the hierarchy, or referred to them speaking "with authority in these supreme matters," it is difficult not to conclude that MDP meant to suggest dogmatic judgments. In these "supreme matters," she said, the Church presents as her evidence something quite different than science or law would present: in fact, the evidences to which the Church might point "are never so logically irresistible that they cannot be controverted." But the Church has a special strength on her side:

> for the facts to which the Church appeals are within our own heart as well as hers; her proofs derive their cogency from the reasonings of our own conscience, and are confirmed by the spiritual needs of which we are conscious. She appeals from the revelation without, which is clearer and more consistent, to the revelation within, which is dimmer indeed and more fitful, but also more intimate and imperative.[29]

The inner dimension, the imperative domain of conscience, religion in its fullest sense – all these concepts recur with frequency throughout this chapter that attempted to delineate spheres of authority within the individual and within the Church. For all their frequency, however, and for their obvious stress on the spiritual rights of the individual within the context of the corporate consciousness of the Church, these concepts are not very concise. When she writes, for instance, that it is an unwelcome truth that "the greatest things of life . . . must be done by ourselves," one is hard pressed to define those "greater things."[30] Even though Maude Petre might insist that such an indeterminateness is written across the face of reality itself, one can only wish that she had made a more detailed attempt to inquire where the great traditional categories (e.g., Scripture, tradition, revelation, dogma) find their place within "religion in its fullest sense." Even the chapter's aphoristic closing words leave uncertainty: "we must render to the Pope and Caesar that which belongs to Pope and Caesar, but to God and our own soul that which is their due."[31] Even after a careful reading of the chapter in question, the reader still wonders: *what* in fact is due to Pope, *what* to Caesar, and *what* to God?

In a chapter of *Catholicism and Independence* entitled "The Fallacy of Undenominationalism" MDP shows up as critic of one of the trends within turn-of-the-century religious liberalism. Although the undenominational, tolerant approach to religion has become widely regarded, it does not always bespeak the noblest attitudes, Maude Petre wrote. If tolerance flows from indifference or from lack of passionate religious commitment, one can hardly be considered to be manifesting a great deal of charity in being silent about truths of which one is half certain.[32] In fact, she indicated, when one does cling to some truth deeply, it is only natural to seek to share that vision of truth with another. Can there be a value, then, in tolerance, in undenominationalism?

Maude Petre looked to a different meaning of the undenominational spirit to find its genuine worth:

> If their meaning is that they are above the narrowness of mere controversy, that their charity will stretch to every form of human misery, that difference of conviction will not close their hearts to any who may need their help, that their own faith will never make them crush the beliefs of others, that their apprehension of truth is too spiritual to allow them to regard any presentation of it as final,

then, however extended their tolerance may be, it is not inconsistent with the most real love for what they regard as vital truth.[33]

On such grounds MDP is able to reach this conclusion: "To be undenominational and consequently tolerant is nothing; but to be denominational in the best sense, and likewise tolerant, is much."[34] Once again, just as the meaning of "religion in the truest sense" was not made absolutely clear, so here "to be denominational in the best sense" is not sufficiently explicated.

Maude Petre's 1907 book that proved so irritating to the authorities concluded with the thought that there are mothers who never allow their children to grow and develop to their fullest capacities. Is the Church such a mother? she wondered. Maude Petre spoke of human parents who too closely guard their children until those children long for a weakening of the tie that binds; she posed the question:

> Have our official rulers fallen into the same mistake as regards a world that has grown up and begins to think for itself? Are they afraid of the best minds amongst their own children?[35]

The question stands unanswered, but not much speculation is needed to predict that Maude Petre's reply would be in the affirmative. She did, however, enumerate the ways in which the Church's children might show themselves worthy offspring of so distinguished a parent:

> If they gather round the table of the sacraments, if they bow their heads and consciences at her tribunal, if they join in her profession of faith, if they accept their assigned place, whether clerical or lay in her hierarchy, if they respect her laws, if they love and protect her little ones, if they bear with the defects of her great ones, if they slake their spiritual thirst at her fountains, have they not proved their parentage better than they would do by any wordy adulation of the action of her authorities?[36]

And having said so much, Maude Petre sealed her case about the loyalty of the Church's questioning children with these warning words: "The children that please and flatter are not always the most faithful in adversity."[37]

The action of Maude Petre's own religious superiors showed that they did not regard her as one of the more faithful children.

The Archbishop of Westminster, as previously noted, asked her to withdraw the book; the London Council of the Daughters of the Heart of Mary refused to permit her to continue under vows in their community. Yet Maude Petre insisted that it was not possible for her to retract.

Catholicism and Independence had been a prophetic call for fearless leaders in the reform of the Church and a manifesto of spiritual independence for those within the Church. For while Maude Petre pointed to the priceless spiritual nourishment that the faithful might receive from the visible Church, she also spoke of the ultimate demands of conscience—admittedly within a corporate context—and of the invisible Church. This invisible Church never received a clear definition or even description within the controversial text, but was somehow identified with the eternal dimensions of religion at its fullest. If *Catholicism and Independence* did not specifically approach any of the major issues of Modernism such as biblical criticism, immanence, or dogmatic development, it did provide a hearty defense of those who might raise such questions.

Meanwhile, the letters of Maude Petre to Anglican Canon A. L. Lilley in 1907, the year of the Modernist explosion, reveal, together with her published writings, the intensity of her commitment to the cause of the Church and the cause of her friends. A particularly impassioned letter was dispatched to Lilley in August 1907, the month between the appearances of the *Lamentabili* (July 4, 1907) and the *Pascendi* (September 8).[38] She wrote:

> The moment is an evil one, and my one wish is that none should lose hope—there are so many amongst us R.C.s who are nearly doing so. For myself, my very belief in my own Church and love for her, make me wish that she might be once more invaded and almost conquered by the best of those outside her, who will join with the best of those within, to bring her, through humiliation, to a truer sense of her own right destiny.
>
> May those amongst us who may be called to a definite line of resistance not lose the love of the cause in the very efforts they will have to make to defend it. . . .[39]

When MDP wrote to Lilley in December, *Pascendi* had already been public for some three months, and she referred to a "real 'reign of terror' in the R. Catholic body." One felt, she wrote, "downright ashamed that such mean and ignorant men should be able to do such harm."[40] But, just as she had expressed a longing in the August letter that a true love of the Church motivate those who pursue the Modernist cause, so now she found hope of growth even in the pain of the 1907 encyclical crisis:

> Well, the night is surely at its darkest, and the day must soon break. But one of the painful elements in the present crisis is that one knows much better what is to go than what is to come. This I can accept as something inevitable to all great movements, only it necessarily makes it harder. My idea is that it is a great and deep movement toward union of some kind. Anyhow, it is surely a privilege to be able to do anything towards it.[41]

By the time she wrote those lines, then, late December 1907, Maude Petre had become painfully aware what the "privilege" of participating in a "great and deep movement towards reunion" would cost her. She could not then be aware, however, of darker days yet to come. The death of George Tyrrell, the dispute over his burial and MDP's executorship of his unpublished writings, her refusal to swear to an anti-Modernist oath, and her subsequent local excommunication—these were all in the very near future. The "cost of discipleship" was to prove very painful indeed.

5

The Death of Tyrrell:

DISCIPLESHIP IN CRISIS

THE YEAR 1908 WAS to prove a kind of lull between two storms for Maude Petre. The previous year had brought the papal encyclical and her severance from her religious community; the succeeding year would see the death of Tyrrell and the beginning of a kind of excommunication for Petre. During this "interim" year of 1908 there appeared the first evidences of her correspondence with Alfred Loisy, a correspondence that would continue until the Frenchman's death in 1940. In a letter of June 21, 1908, she described herself to Loisy as a lover of truth but not a scholar. In the same letter she told Loisy that though she was not badly upset by a change in the concept of dogma, a change in the value of scriptural facts themselves was quite a different matter. But, she concluded, the only solution to the problem of criticism is to seek the truth without fear.[1]

As part of her own truth seeking, Maude Petre late in 1908 had done a short article in Italian for the periodical *Nova et Vetera* published at Rome.[2] Entitled "Ossequio o idolatria?" the essay examined the exaggerations and extravagances of respect for the pope urged by a short book, *Devotion au pape*, which had been written by Arsene Milet and published with an imprimatur in 1904. Pointing out that her own English Catholic forebears could never have understood such excesses, MDP expressed a desire to be loyal to a pope who did not look on the faithful as a mere slavish lot. She insisted that the papal office was meant for the faithful, and not the faithful for the office.[3]

The pope, she wrote, should help people to come to God, but he should not take the place of God in the human heart. Furthermore, she decried the semi-divine status accorded the pontiff by many Catholics, especially from the sixteenth century onward. And for good measure, Maude Petre suggested an imagined Ignatian meditation that would be appropriate to those who make an idol of the pope. Such people should pray to the pope, she gibed; and she suggested this prayer:

> O heart of the Holy Father . . . warm my heart, Make me love what you love — make me love the heretics and Modernists in the manner you love them, and in no other way.[4]

Obviously, despite this tongue-in-cheek example of prayer, Maude Petre did *not* feel toward Modernists as did the pope and bishops. In fact, MDP recorded in her diary in 1908 a confrontation with her own bishop, Peter Amigo of the Southwark Diocese, about her friendship with Modernists.

In 1906–7 Maude Petre had begun planning to take a house in the small Sussex village of Storrington. It was her hope to found there a convalescent home,[5] and she eventually readied a two-room cottage on the rear of the property for George Tyrrell's use. Tyrrell was living in these rooms late in 1908 when Bishop Amigo came to the village of Storrington, part of the jurisdiction of the Diocese of Southwark at that time. The Prior of the local Catholic Priory church — staffed by Premonstratensian Fathers — had already asked Petre to tell the excommunicated Tyrrell that he was not welcome at Storrington.[6] Then Bishop Amigo informed her that he too objected to her receiving Modernists in her home.[7] Maude Petre seemed to hold to the old theory of the Englishman's home being his castle: Tyrrell remained.

Shortly after the incident with Bishop Amigo, MDP traveled to Italy and there met Italian Modernists Ernesto Buonaiuti (1881–1946) and Antonio Fogazzaro (1842–1911). While at Rome, she had met with the Marquise des Monstiers, whom she described as "intensely bitter against the Church." MDP recorded that she was attempting to rouse the faith of the Marquise in the invisible Church. Apparently this Marquise des Monstiers was the one-time friend of Bishop John Lancaster Spalding of Peoria. The Marquise, the former Mary Gwendolen Caldwell of Louisville, had at Bishop Spalding's urging contributed $300,000 toward the construction of Catholic University of America in 1885. She had been living in Europe after her marriage to a French Marquis, and partly disillusioned by the lack of sanctity she saw in the European Church, she left the Catholic Church in 1904. In October of 1909, the same year that Petre had visited with her, the Marquise died.[8] On her way back to England late in February 1909, Maude noted in her diary that she was "hopeful in spite of all. Men like Fogazzaro make one feel that the fight is not for nought."[9]

The great issues of the Church were soon to be eclipsed for Maude Petre for awhile, however. For in July 1909 came sudden and unexpected personal tragedy—the death of George Tyrrell. Maude described the death of her friend as "of one passing forth from the little known to the less known; but passing forth in trust as well as fear."[10]

Tyrrell's last illness began on July 6, with one of his frequent severe headaches, and for two days the grave nature of his affliction was not realized. But paralysis began to set in, as well as indistinct speech. Maude, however, insisted that "Tyrrell's mind was clear from first to last,"[11] except for periods of semi-consciousness and coma. As the serious nature of the illness became apparent, Maude Petre was faced with the difficult question of Tyrrell's reception of last sacraments. She considered Tyrrell too weak and in too much pain to consult him, and it was she who decided the question. She sought to prevent ecclesiastical pressure on Tyrrell; at the same time she wanted him to have a priest, since he might not be fully aware of his own danger, and so could die without spiritual comfort. On July 9, Maude consulted Baron von Hügel, and together they decided to summon a priest.[12]

Father Charles L. Dessoulavy came on the tenth, heard Tyrrell's confession and gave him conditional absolution. Tyrrell remarked afterward to Maude, "He won't let me die without the Sacraments."[13] There was a brief rally in Tyrrell's condition; then a sudden turn on July 12 convinced Maude Petre that she must have a priest in for Extreme Unction. Because Dessoulavy could not be reached in time, she called most reluctantly on the Prior, Xavier de le Fourvière, who had considered Tyrrell *persona non grata*. The Prior did come to anoint Tyrrell, and the dying man extended his hand to receive the sacramental oil, Maude Petre would later insist when the question became disputed. The Prior asked if he might return to visit the patient the next day; Petre responded that he could not. It was on the same day, July 12, that Bremond arrived and also heard Tyrrell's confession.[14]

On July 13, a Jesuit priest, J. Hungerford Pollen, came, asking to see Tyrrell. When Maude asked the reason for the visit, Pollen would give no response; accordingly she told Pollen that he could not see Tyrrell alone and accompanied him into the dying man's room.[15] As Tyrrell was unconscious, Pollen's visit – whatever its intention – was apparently futile. Italian papers had speculated that Tyrrell had expressed regret for his "apostacy" to the Jesuits. Later, some of the papers reported that he had not even been admitted to Tyrrell's room. Maude Petre tersely reported: "Both reports were false."[16]

George Tyrrell's life was not to end, however, without a touch of personal – as well as ecclesiastical – drama. Tyrrell had at least two close female friends in addition to Maude Petre – Norah Shelley and Katherine Clutton. Neither was particularly well-disposed to MDP.[17]

As Tyrrell neared his last hours, according to MDP's rather candid diary accounts, Norah Shelley arrived for the death vigil, augmenting the company of von Hügel, Bremond, MDP herself, her sister Mrs. Sweetman Powell, and Tyrrell's cousin, William Tyrrell.[18] Shortly before the Shelley arrival, Maude Petre had been able to report that in Tyrrell's last hours he displayed what must have been an unusual tenderness. She had reported on July 8 "first kiss"! And four days later "He put his arm round me so lovingly he drew my face down and kissed me on each cheek and on the mouth."

When Norah Shelley appeared on the scene, however, "trouble began" in Maude's own phrase. Of July 13, MDP wrote in her diary: "cannot remember much – a weary struggle with Norah Shelley who was the haunting horror of it all . . . telling people he cared more for her than for anyone . . . pressing herself on his notice."

But, the final triumph in this small personal sidelight of life and death among the Modernists was Maude Petre's. She wrote:

> Suddenly [Tyrrell] started up, looked at me and threw out his arm to me, I went to him and he put it round me. I spoke to him. Norah Shelley tried to push herself between – but, thank God, she could not entirely destroy that last moment.[19]

On the morning of July 15, 1909, then, around nine o'clock, George Tyrrell died. MDP lamented in particular that his best theological work might still have been ahead of him. And yet, echoing Tennyson, she wrote to A. L. Lilley: "But, if one cannot trust the larger hope then everything is so utterly worthless that even sorrow itself would become a trifling thing."[20]

That same day of Tyrrell's death, Maude Petre sent letters to both the *Times* and the *Daily Mail* in an attempt to prevent any misunderstanding that Tyrrell might have "recanted." As she wrote the letters, she was in possession of a personal testament Tyrrell had attached to his will. This testament said in part, "I wish to give no basis for the rumor that I made any sort of retraction of those Catholic principles which I defended against the Vatican heresies."[21] Accordingly, this letter appeared in the papers over Maude Petre's signature the day after Tyrrell's death:

> To obviate any danger of false reports, I am anxious to give you promptly certain details regarding the last days of Father George Tyrrell, who died in my house this morning.
>
> He was taken suddenly ill on Tuesday, the 6th, and became at once partly inarticulate, although I myself could distinguish a good deal of what he said up to nearly the end.
>
> When his condition became graver I decided, on July 10th, in accordance with my own views and those of Baron Friedrich von Hügel, to send for a priest of the diocese of Southwark, one of his friends.
>
> This priest being assured by us that, on account of the physical condition of Father Tyrrell, he could come to no clear understanding with him, had recourse previously to the evidence and testimony of Baron von Hügel, who perfectly knew the general line of thought and could interpret the present dispositions of the sick man.
>
> In answer to his questions, the Baron was able to reply that, according to his certain knowledge (1) Father Tyrrell would wish to receive all the rites of the Church; (2) he would be deeply contrite for all and any sin or excess of which he had been guilty, as in other matters so in the course of controversy, but (3) he would not wish to receive the sacraments at the cost of a retraction of what he had said and written in all sincerity, and still considered to be the truth. The aforesaid priest acknowledged his clear

understanding of these points, and then proceeded to the interview. Father Tyrrell talked at some length, probably making a confession, after which he received conditional absolution. On Monday, the 12th, his condition became so much graver that it seemed advisable to have no further delay, such as would have been necessitated by sending again for the same priest. I therefore asked the Prior of Storrington to come and give Extreme Unction, Communion being out of the question, owing to the absence of the power to swallow. He came at once, and performed the Sacred Rites in my presence, Father Tyrrell being conscious. On the 12th, his intimate friend, Abbé Bremond, arrived and had the opportunity, in a moment of very clear consciousness that evening, of speaking to him, accepting such confession as he could express by signs, and giving him a last absolution. He also attended him to his very last moment.[22]

This letter to the *Times* proved a stumbling block in the battle that immediately ensued over a Catholic burial for George Tyrrell. Two of the principal combatants in the dispute had been in confrontation before: Bishop Peter Amigo and Maude Petre; nor was this to be the last of their disagreements. Bishop Amigo had written the Prior of Storrington the day of Tyrrell's death: "I am not satisfied about him. I wish he could have retracted. Before deciding on the funeral, kindly let me have all particulars."[23] Maude Petre's letter had made it fairly clear that no retraction had been made. The scene was set for conflict over Tyrrell's burial.

On the sixteenth, the day that MDP's letter appeared in the *Times*, Bishop Amigo wrote to her that unless either Father Bremond or Father Dessoulavy could assure him in writing that Tyrrell had retracted, a Catholic burial was out of the question. MDP replied by telegram:

Think my duty respectfully to warn your Lordship scandal of your refusal will be enormous to numbers in and outside Church. What you ask was impossible in case of speechless and weak man. Canonical right to burial since he received Sacraments. Should spare nothing to explain all in Press if refusal maintained.[24]

On July 18 came word that Catholic burial might be possible at Brentwood under the jurisdiction of the Archbishop of Westminster. The following day, Maude Petre and Henri Bremond went up to London to discuss the case. They asked to see Archbishop Bourne but were told by "two ecclesiastics" that he was not at home. Maude apparently felt that she and Bremond were being put off. She and Bremond argued with the clerics on what she called "strictly ecclesiastical lines."

> We did not argue whether his whole life had been right or wrong; what we argued was that he should be treated as others were treated. Therefore, we said, "He received the Sacraments." They answered, "He made no recantation." We replied not that he ought not or ought to have done so, but that he was "physically unable." They said, "How about that letter you wrote to the papers." I replied, "it was I wrote it and not he—it does not alter what he did." Nothing was to be gained and we left the Archbishop's house, I warning them that I would have an answer from the Archbishop and accept nothing else.[25]

MDP and Bremond then went to see Bishop Amigo, whom she described as "a very suave prelate." "But his words," she added, "go beyond his deeds." A Jesuit priest, Sydney Smith was present at the interview with Bishop Amigo and kept referring to the scandal that would arise from a Catholic burial for Tyrrell. Maude "silenced him sharply each time by remarking that his Lordship would be quite above such cowardly considerations."

Despite Maude Petre's appeal and the entreaties of Tyrrell's own relatives, Amigo's judgment remained firm. As he expressed it in a terse wire to Tyrrell's cousin, William Tyrrell:

> Extremely sorry but not personal matter, though feeble Tyrrell should have made some retraction which could now be published. Unless he retracted Catholic Burial impossible.

William Tyrrell, for his part, wrote back to Bishop Amigo that he found the prelate's judgment "unnecessarily harsh."[26]

At last, burial was arranged to take place in a corner of the Anglican parish cemetary at Storrington on July 21. Henri Bremond spoke a eulogy over Tyrrell's grave, for which he was temporarily suspended from saying Mass.[27]

Why did such turmoil arise from a simple burial? Maude Petre anticipated the question herself, and her response gives yet another glimpse of her own approach to the Church and Catholicism:

Now some wonder why we worked so hard to obtain a Catholic funeral. I venture to think it was our duty to do so. Not to have done so would have been to give the lie to his life, *and to accept the notion that official, sectarian, ultramontane Catholicism was true Catholicism.*[28]

Maude Petre's attempt to defend George Tyrrell's position did not cease with his burial. A letter written in French by the Prior of Storrington, signed F. Xavier, C.R.P., appeared in the *Tablet* of July 24. In assessing what is called Maude Petre's "deplorable" letter to the *Times*, the letter of the Prior went through a twenty-one point discussion, charging that she had not correctly assessed his own role in "this sad circumstance." For example, the Prior noted that he had written Petre on July 11 expressing concern for Tyrrell and had received a card in reply saying that he was not welcome. Further, he suggested that she and the Baron had set themselves up as keepers of Tyrrell's soul and intimated that Tyrrell with "his high intelligence and great heart" might have retracted had it not been for Petre and von Hügel.[29]

The *Tablet* of July 31 brought replies both from Baron von Hügel (whom the Prior had guessed in his letter was a co-author of the earlier letter) and from Maude Petre herself. Von Hügel wrote that the Prior was correct in his assumption that he had collaborated with Petre in composing the letter. He then continued:

But our haste in publishing such a declaration was certainly not to prevent the truth about Fr. Tyrrell's dispositions during the time of his indubitable lucidity of mind and about the circumstances of his death from being known, but, on the contrary, to impede the formation of a legend. . . .

As for his insinuations concerning the motives of Miss Petre and myself, I would say but two words. Anybody who knows either her or myself knows also that we are utterly incapable of what the Prior has suggested. And those who do not know us, know, at least, that such grave accusations require proof.[30]

Maude Petre's letter to the *Tablet* charged that the Prior's letter erred "chiefly in its suppression of a most important and previous fact." Maude then related the incident in which the Prior had deeply hurt Father Tyrrell by telling him that he was an unwelcome person in Storrington.[31]

Maude Petre persisted in asking why Tyrrell was treated differently from others in the matter of burial. What other cases had there been, she asked, "in which the Sacraments have been administered and received with evident willingness and Catholic burial refused afterward?"[32]

Then, in September 1909, MDP counseled her old friend Henri Bremond to make an anti-Modernist declaration demanded of him. The Holy See wanted Bremond to ask Bishop Amigo's pardon for having prayed and spoken at Tyrrell's grave and to give an adherence to *Pascendi* and *Lamentabili*. Bremond wrote Petre about this on September 8, 1909, and asked, "being professedly a Catholic, can I refuse publicly to adhere to pontifical utterances?" In effect, he placed the decision in Maude's hands, urging her to "wire . . . either *stop* or *go on*" with his submission.[33]

Maude Petre did not hesitate to urge Bremond to submit his letter containing a dogmatic submission coupled with an expression of ongoing love for his friend Tyrrell.[34] Did such advice represent a contradiction in Maude Petre's approach? Actually, it was in accord with the acknowledgment of varieties of response possible to the encyclical to which she would refer in her famous letter to the *Times* of November 2, 1910. But more specifically in the case of Bremond, Maude had an explanation which she offered in a letter to A. L. Lilley:

> I cannot tell you how much I dreaded the prospect of his being forced into Fr. Tyrrell's position; the martyrdom that was an essential element in the career of the former would be perfectly futile in that of the latter. Père Bremond is not a Modernist nor seriously interested in Modernist questions. . . . No other Church would have the least attraction for him, and it would be deadly to his Catholic influence, and unfortunate for his own religious welfare, to be without Church or sacraments or communion with any body of the faithful.[35]

In a will Tyrrell had written in 1905, he made Maude Petre his literary executor.[36] Accordingly, one of her immediate tasks was the publication of Tyrrell's *Christianity at the Cross-Roads*,[37] which he had written shortly before his death. The book traced out Tyrrell's reaction to the charges of Modernism; it examined in some detail both the scholarship about the historical Jesus and the development of the reality of Jesus in the Church, sharply contrasting Catholic Modernism with Protestant liberalism. Maude Petre herself seemed to consider *Christianity at the Cross-Roads* Tyrrell's most accomplished work.[38]

The greater part of Tyrrell's work is devoted to a critical study of the biblical figure of Jesus, with special emphasis on Jesus' sense of apocalyptic. While this might have been a hearty refutation to the mild-mannered, moralistic Jesus of Protestant liberalism, it also raised critical questions as to Jesus' knowledge and his ongoing Beatific Vision. Maude Petre would describe the Christ of *Christianity at the Cross-Roads* in these words of her biographical study of Tyrrell:

> It is not, then, the Christ of theological subtleties that we find in "Christianity at the Cross-Roads;" but it is the Christ of Catholic faith and worship; the Christ who labours with man as his yoke-fellow, sharing his struggles, his disappointments, his darkness, his ignorance; a partner in his sorrows, but more than a partner in his faith and his hope.[39]

The publication of Tyrrell's writings—especially those that might speak of ignorance and darkness in the human life of Jesus—certainly did not strengthen Petre's popularity with the hierarchy. Church authority had already extracted from Henri Bremond a kind of apology for his part in the Tyrrell burial.[40] It is Loisy's implication that the bishop now sought some similar sign from Maude Petre. In fact, Loisy interpreted Bishop Amigo's eagerness to get Maude to sign an act of submission to *Lamentabili* and *Pascendi* as an attempt to prevent her publication of Tyrrell's life.[41]

This much, however, is fact rather than interpretation: before 1909 ended, Church authority turned to a means other than verbal persuasion in its disciplinary stance toward Petre. It would make her feel more keenly still the cost of her allegiance to Tyrrell and to her religious convictions by invoking against her one of the Church's oldest disciplines: she was refused the reception of Communion by her bishop.

6

The Cost of Allegiance:

SACRAMENTAL AND LITERARY CLASHES

EARLY IN DECEMBER 1909 Maude Petre wrote her friend A. L. Lilley the details on an incident that had occurred in the Priory church at Storrington on December 2:

> Just at communion time when I was rising to go up, the Prior rushed into the Church, came up to me and asked "Have you received my letter?" I answered in great astonishment, "No!" . . . "You cannot go to Communion," he said. I said, "Did the Bishop say so?" "No, but you cannot." I said, "You have no right to stop me." He said, "If you go up I will go and stop the priest." I said, "I will not make a scandal, but I deny your right and you will suffer for it." This conversation in the middle of the Church which was not empty. . . . [1]

She then went on to explain to Lilley how isolated she felt her plight to be within Catholicism. To whom could she turn for advice within her own Church? Maude wrote:

> Of course I have company outside my own Church; and after all these distinctions become very unimportant to me as time goes on. Only, in fact, no one under the same yoke has had to solve just the same question.[2]

One immediate recourse Maude Petre had taken within her own Church, however, was to write Bishop Amigo. In a letter of December 7, 1909, the bishop had told Miss Petre that she could help him in resolving the problem between the Prior and herself by declaring her allegiance to *Pascendi* and *Lamentabili*.[3] In response, Maude had written Bishop Amigo and expressed her own kind of allegiance to the faith:

> As to my own faith, I adhere to that in which I was educated from childhood when I was instructed in the Catholic creed, but taught far more of the duties and practices of Catholic life than of any theological subtleties. If, therefore, my life does not testify to my faith, I think my signature would be entirely vain.

She then referred specifically to the papal documents about Modernism:

> I only read the "Lamentabili" and "Pascendi" once, and that a long time ago. They made on me a very painful impression which I found was shared by a great many Catholics; for they seemed to condemn writers like Cardinal Newman and Father Tyrrell who had been our greatest Catholic apologists; they seemed to hamper the mind in the acceptance of scientific and historical facts; the Pascendi seemed to advocate a line of conduct contrary to general notions of charity. If I am wrong in this I shall be very glad to be convinced of my error.[4]

Two days later the Bishop of Southwark replied to his subject. Because he once again made the reception of the Eucharist dependent on Maude's acceptance of *Pascendi*, and because Maude herself was not inclined to relent, the lines of impasse were firmly drawn.[5]

The following month, January 1910, Maude Petre, having seen the turmoil surrounding Tyrrell's burial while under excommunication, prepared a private testament for her family in the event a similar fate should befall her. In it, she described her own situation in this way: "I am under a kind of partial, local pseudo-excommunication." Although she expressed an eagerness to die with the sacraments, she expressly forbid the ministration of any priest of Storrington Priory; but should some other priest be aware of her views and not be put in any jeopardy by attending to her, then, she said, she would be very happy to receive the Sacraments, ". . . which I value, perhaps as deeply as those who have refused them to me." She then wrote words that bear a kind of epic ring, words that might have been spoken by a Joan of Arc, a Martin Luther, a Thomas More:

> If I am wrong, then I am so deeply, fundamentally wrong, that only God can prove it to me. If I am right, then He will make good to me what I have forfeited before men.

Fresh from the experience of Bremond's suspension after Tyrrell's burial, Maude asked that no priest attend her graveside, and should any be inclined to attend, she asked them to say a Mass for her instead. She noted the prayers she wished to be said during the burial—including the Nicene Creed to be prayed over the grave itself. She concluded the document with a tribute to George Tyrrell:

> Being now in full possession of my ordinary faculties, I desire to say that I regard it as a privilege to have been able to work for Fr. Tyrrell's memory: that I would gladly do more than I am doing, had I the requisite ability: that I think God raised him up in spite of all his faults, to do a great work for the future of the Church: that I believe he was a martyr in the cause for which he labored. All my views have not been the same as his, but the more independent my mind, the deeper can be the reverence in which I held and continue to hold him.[6]

On the whole, then, Maude Petre seemed resigned to her ecclesiastical status, and it might have simply remained so indefinitely.[7] But new complications soon arose. She had been refused Communion in the Priory church at Storrington and the bishop would not order the Prior to allow her to communicate; but Maude Petre felt free to receive Communion at other churches in the diocese. The bishop wrote her, accordingly, in October 1910, that he had heard that she was, in fact, receiving Communion, and that until she submitted in matters of faith to papal authority, she was forbidden Communion throughout his diocese. The "pseudo-excommunication" (as Maude herself had called it) was thus spread beyond the boundary of one parish. The bishop closed his letter with this wish: "God grant that you may realize your position and submit to the authority of the Vicar of Christ."[8]

But Maude Petre was in no mood to submit; in fact, she asked the bishop for a letter to show around to clear her of any accusation of receiving Communion against his order, since the order had only just been given. This letter, Maude Petre said, she must have "in fairness to my character for uprightness and loyalty; I have acted quite above board and have concealed nothing from you." In conclusion, Maude threatened a publication of the history of their dispute if such a clearance was not forthcoming from the bishop.[9]

Another set of letters was exchanged. Bishop Amigo wrote Petre again on October 11: "Assure me that you are not a modernist; make your profession of faith before me, and the prohibition will at once be removed."[10] In reply, MDP wrote a very long letter on October 14, asking why she alone of all lay people should be asked to express herself on the papal documents. She concluded with a kind of challenge to the bishop: She asked him to explain why a pronouncement that is not *de fide* should call for such a solemn commitment as does the Creed.[11]

But it was at this point that the dispute left the realm of private correspondence. Maude Petre incorporated the letter of October 14 to Amigo into an even longer "Open Letter to My Fellow Catholics" that appeared in the *Times* of London on November 2, 1910. It represented both Maude Petre's most studied written reaction to the encyclical on Modernism as well as one of the most inflammatory actions of resistance to the document in the Church. The *Revue Moderniste Internationale* published a French translation with the wish that Maude Petre's action would "stir a great flame."[12] The letter also appeared in print in Italian in the journal *Coenobium* with the comment that Miss Petre showed herself more virile than most men in her stance.[13] And Loisy commented that had all those obliged to take the oath against Modernism responded as she had, Rome would have been forced to forego the oath altogether.[14]

The letter to the *Times* opened with Maude Petre's acknowledgment that she, having no official authority, and being "a woman with no advanced theories in regard to my sex, and little disposed, as my past testifies, to public life or action" should write such a letter. But she now found herself in a singular position, she said, in that Church authority was trying to compel her to pronounce on "documents with regard to which I have never made any public utterance."

Catholics, Maude thought, have not enough sympathy for that priest who must either reject the submission to the encyclical and face an end to his career and consequent poverty, or accept the submission, thereby "violating his own higher instincts and helping the policy of repression." The laity, often failing to grasp the depth of suffering these priests undergo, should not too harshly judge "certain expedients" that they may take. Each of these men, in the absence of any organization "stands or falls alone." They will continue alone in their plight unless they form some organization, "or unless public opinion comes to the rescue." She noted that "old-fashioned" Catholics had not been called upon to subscribe to Church documents. Apparently making yet another reference to the old English Catholics, she suspected that had such men "been asked to sign professions of the faith which was to them a matter of daily practice, they would have answered with more energy than sweetness that they had never departed from the faith and did not need to prove it."

That type of Catholic may not now be dominant, Petre admitted, but the modern Catholic, while remaining faithful to the Church's recognized authority, should "have surely enough independence left to . . . object to anything in the nature of tyranny." She then proceeded to recount her own communication and declaration to Church authority on the subject of adherence to the encyclical.

There are, she allowed, three ways in which any person might show adherence to the papal documents in question. The first is the path that would accept any declaration "leaving all responsibility for the objective truth or subjective honesty of such a declaration on the shoulders of one's superiors." In its extreme form, this would be counted "an act of blind obedience." Some, MDP noted, find such a course legitimate and necessary to prevent scandal. This course may be "ideally unsatisfactory," but she would not condemn those who responded in such a way. This would never, however, be her own position. "I am not in a position of importance," she wrote, "and can follow the dictates of my conscience regardless of all public considerations."

The second manner of adherence MDP also rejected for herself: "the manner of a theologian." This approach was considered even less acceptable because of its attempts at "explaining, qualifying, distinguishing various meanings." To all such attempts, she reacted strongly: "the decree and encyclical must be taken in the sense which the Pope obviously gives to them or not at all."

In coming to the third approach, Maude Petre came to the central thrust and challenge of her letter:

> Therefore there remains, for myself, but one way of making such a declaration and that is to declare that I accept these docu-

ments, *and actually to accept them, inwardly and outwardly* in their meaning as their *words*, from the first line to the last.

This would be a solemn action and before giving your Lordship my answer, which shall be a truthful one, I hope I may, without presumption, ask one question—viz.: will your Lordship assure me, on your episcopal authority, that every condemnation or proposition of those 2 documents, without a single exception is *de fide* now, and will always be in the same sense *de fide.*

I quite understand that there might be other duties of silence and respect towards pronouncements not *de fide*; but here I am asked for more than respect or silence. I am asked for such an act of solemn adhesion as I gave, by proxy, in baptism, and on other occasions in person, to articles of faith; and I hold that if I am to give this act of adhesion I must be ready, with God's grace, to lay down my life under tortures, should such a crisis occur, for the least word of these documents as for the Apostle's Creed.

If the authority of the Church is unwilling to answer her question with a "clear affirmative," she thought, then they clearly demand that the faithful commit themselves more solemnly "than do those in authority who make the demand of us." Besides, she continued, echoing sentiments from her 1907 book *Catholicism and Independence*—now taken from the abstract and applied to the particular—there is no assurance that the hierarchy will not exceed the limits of their power. And if they do so, "every form of resistance is not *ipso facto* unlawful." In an age when the State so highly values freedom, all the more is it said to be appropriate to plead for those confronted with submission to the encyclical, "some of the most earnest and intelligent of our clergy." "Perhaps," she wrote in conclusion, "among our Bishops some might be glad to see a firm, though loyal resistance opposed to a system, which is humiliating local Sees and crushing the life out of local churches."[15]

One of the first responses MDP received to her volley came, unexpectedly, from Arthur Conan Doyle of Sherlock Holmes fame. Doyle wrote that he admired "the quiet resolution and excellent logic" of her letter, but noted that he had already gone "through and past" her position. Still, as one now outside the Church, he could look on with sympathy for her plight as one trying to be faithful to an institution that is "cracking in all directions." Doyle figured that if the Roman Catholic Church was to be saved, it could only be through such liberal sentiments as those of MDP. And yet Doyle lamented that the only use the Church could presently find for those who held such positions was "to chase them out."[16]

Catholic reaction to Maude Petre's letter was not so friendly. In a three-column editorial entitled "A Regrettable Letter," the *Tablet* took Maude Petre to task. Miss Petre, the editorial noted, had posed the question why she alone should be singled out to sign submission to papal documents and be refused Communion for noncompliance. The *Tablet* allowed that it would be un-chivalrous for the hierarchy to single out a woman in such fashion — especially "the daughter of one of those historic Catholic families of the land that have suffered much for the faith and merited well of the Church" — without very good reason. Additionally, Maude Petre in particular "has a record, which is not forgotten, of deeds of generosity and charity." Is there, then, good reason to be found for the attitude and action of her bishop?

Yes, the editorial insisted, Bishop Amigo stood on firm ground. Through her friendship with Tyrrell, Maude Petre had furthered the Modernist cause. She had published Tyrrell's posthumous book (*Christianity at the Cross-Roads*) "which in spirit and import deviated in no substantial degree from his former Modernist teaching." Far from repudiating his stance that had been condemned by the authorities, Tyrrell had re-presented it; and in his letter to "old Catholic" Bishop Edward Herzog, of Berne, Tyrrell had rejected the Councils of Trent and the Vatican as well as papal primacy. By presenting this work of Tyrrell to the world, the *Tablet* said, Maude Petre "placed herself publicly in sympathy with a system which has been solemnly condemned by the Holy See as the synthesis of all heresies."

For the rest, the editorial declared that if one were un-Catholic enough to oppose the pope, that same one should refrain from Holy Communion. And, the editorial further claimed, Rome can claim allegiance not only in matters of faith, "but to those things which are of necessity involved in and required by the holding and defense of the Faith."[17]

The following week's edition of the *Tablet* brought a reply from Petre. She said that it was not possible "to adhere *with one's whole soul* to any statement of whose entire and lasting truth one is not absolutely certain and convinced." She maintained that it would be "very difficult for those aware of the latest acquirements in church history and scripture science to sign unconditionally . . . certain parts of the papal documents."[18]

The *Tablet* added a lengthy editor's note at the foot of Petre's letter. It referred her to the documents of the First Vatican Council urging Catholics to reject not only heresy but also errors proximate to it. The first five articles of the formula of the Oath against Modernism are said to cut the groundwork from under Modernism and "assent is required to these as taught by the infallible magisterium of the Church."[19]

Although Maude Petre eventually moved to London in the Diocese of Westminster and there received Communion daily,[20] she continued to be troubled by her unusual status with the Southwark Diocese. It is remarkable to note that for thirty years she sought to normalize her sacramental status. The story is long, and somewhat painful; it will not be recounted here.[21] In all likelihood, Petre's persistence both in refusing the anti-Modernist oath and in receiving Communion in the Roman Catholic Church was based on the same exigency that drove her to insist on a Catholic burial for Tyrrell; it would validate her hope that her "way of faith" was genuinely Catholic. As late as 1939, when Pius XII became pope, Maude Petre wrote to him and received from his Secretary of State a courteous, noncommittal reply.[22]

If Maude Petre was uneasy with her ecclesiastical position, in the first years after Tyrrell's death, however, she did not let it interfere with the work she felt called to do. She set to work on the biography of George Tyrrell. Her deceased friend had entrusted his autobiographical writings to her before his death, but the autobiographical section only extended as far as 1885; from that point onward Maude had to take up the writing herself.[23]

The Autobiography and Life of George Tyrrell, a lengthy, two-volume study that eventually found its way onto the Index of Forbidden Books, appeared in 1912.[24] For her own intense involvement in its writings, Maude Petre was privately termed "a sinful woman" by the Holy Office in Rome.

Truth to tell, in the *Autobiography and Life* MDP reiterated many of Tyrrell's well-known and controversial positions. There was, for instance, the reintroduction of a theological challenge to

the eternity of hell.[25] In addition Tyrrell's antipathy to the monar-
chical papacy found very strong expression. "Vaticanism," the
troubled Jesuit had written, is now an "outworn and mischievous
frame-work of Catholicism." "Rome," he said, "cares nothing for
religion — only for power."[26] He also denied the ecumenical
authority of the Council of Trent and Vatican I.[27]

MDP involved herself not only by objectively reporting
George Tyrrell's beliefs; she went on at times to defend her
friend's approach. Faced with Tyrrell's attacks on the papacy, for
instance, she reminded her readers that Dante, Catherine of Siena,
and Robert Bellarmine had all also attacked excesses in the
papacy.[28] She also compared George Tyrrell's protest favorably
to those of Martin Luther. The German reformer, MDP argued,
supported his challenges to authority by claiming that he had no
choice: *Ich kann nicht anders*. Tyrrell, she thought, would have
been in a similar position because "this was the answer the prophet
always must give."[29]

The fact that Maude Petre had published such a work,
presenting once again Tyrrell's major theological positions, drew
new anger down upon her own head. Far from taking general
issue with Tyrrell, she had cast him in the role of the prophet. The
Roman reaction, as already noted, was predictable enough: the
volumes were placed on the Index. In the United States, the Jesuit
magazine *America* devoted two sentences to the nearly one-
thousand-page enterprise that Henri Bremond had predicted
would be "one of the world's greatest autobiographies."[30] Tyrrell's
positions had been "reaffirmed and defended." *America* reported:
"We of course cannot commend it to our readers."[31] An appreciative, twenty-page review article by Alfred Fawkes (who had
returned to the Church of England himself after being a Roman
Catholic priest)[32] appeared in the *Quarterly Review* early in 1913.
He spoke of Miss Petre's "candour" and "detachment" and commented that "seldom had so worthy a monument been raised by
a friend to a friend."[33]

With the publication of the *Autobiography and Life of George
Tyrrell* in 1912, a certain phase in Maude Petre's life can be said
to have drawn to a close. Although she would still publish Tyrrell's *Essays on Faith and Immortality*[34] in 1914 and a collection of
his *Letters* in 1920,[35] by the time of the First World War, her

direct "stewardship" of Tyrrell was drawing to a close. She would, of course, continue to write and lecture about George Tyrrell, and as indicated already, she would feel his strong influence in her own life to its very end.

But a new kind of life was beginning for Maude Petre. She was separated from her religious community and forbidden to receive Communion in the Southwark Diocese. Tyrrell was dead and the thrust of the Modernist movement itself had all but died under the papal reaction. Alec Vidler has noted that later years would see Maude Petre and Ernesto Buonaiuti as the only original Modernists in whom the Modernist spirit remained alive and active. He noted that Miss Petre had spoken of herself in 1922 as "a solitary, marooned passenger; the sole living representative of what has come to be regarded as a lost cause—the cause of Modernism in the Roman Catholic Church."[36]

But Petre herself never considered the cause entirely a lost one. The three decades through which she lived after the publication of the *Autobiography and Life of George Tyrrell* were years in which she sought new directions for what she considered the central moving force of Modernism: "a reform of the Church as well as a new understanding of her so that the Church shall be subservient to the religious and spiritual needs of humanity."[37] Her own deepened sense of humanity's spiritual needs account for many of the new themes that would appear in Maude Petre's postwar writings. In addition to her historical analyses of Modernism, she wrote on her own experiences and her reflections concerning both the suffering of war and the need for wider international understanding.

7

War and Peace

As the Modernist drama was being played out within the Catholic Church, terrible and hostile forces were gathering across the face of Europe. The illusions of inevitable progress that had been a mainstay of nineteenth-century life were already reeling down a precipitous slide that would plummet at last into the morass of the World War, the "war to end all wars." The First World War would become, in fact, such a dividing point in modern experience and perception that the world after it would be changed utterly.[1] The characters involved in the Modernist movement within Catholicism could not help but be drawn into the wider vortex of social and spiritual issues raised by such civilizational turmoil.

Maude Petre had involved herself after 1910 with an annual parley devoted to a consideration of spirituality and society held in the abandoned abbey of Pontigny in the Yonne district of France. The abbey had been purchased years earlier by Paul Desjardins, who also deeply involved himself in the annual conversations. Loisy, as well, took part in these events, which he later recounted were intended to address contemporary society's harsh competitiveness, economic servitude and reluctance of its members to be of service to others.[2] In 1914, the very year the World War began, MDP noted after the conference: "Pontigny was wonderful . . . the love and reverence of all—those with faith and those without—a triumph of goodness and love."[3]

In the prewar years Maude Petre did not limit her concern to social questions alone, of course. She had given a paper in mid-1913 to the International Congress of Religious Progress at Paris; it was published the following year as "The Advantages and Disadvantages of Authority in Religion" and amounted to yet

68

another defense of an obedience that allowed the individual to exercise "self-donation to greater than private ends."[4]

It is in the Catholic Church, the essay contended, that "we have experienced not only the worst, but also the best of which authority is capable."[5] Fresh from her own battles with ecclesiastical power structures, MDP contended that a great religious movement can flourish only if authority remains both respected and limited. There can be, in effect, a principle of *limited obedience* that saves the individual from ecclesiastical anarchism: "If men could learn to obey, and to obey wholeheartedly, but no farther, would not authority be, *ipso facto*, forced into its proper dimensions?"[6]

By autumn of 1914, Britons were furious over the Prussian invasion of Belgium. In September, Maude Petre opened her home to Belgian refugees.[7] In October 1914 she wrote another of her letters to the *Times*, this one called "Let Us Be English"; it was directed against excessive persecution of the "German arch-enemies."[8]

By March of 1915 MDP was in France in a nursing capacity at the war hospital set up at Pontigny. Like many others in these years, she found herself nearly overwhelmed with the all-pervading sense of evil and desolation. She confided to her diary, "more and more feel that this world is a sad place to live in . . . one [must] more and more cling to the simple, and to animals as the nearest to unspoilt life."[9] As if to prove her point, Petre rushed from the front back to London when she received wires informing her of the grave illness of her own dog Ben. The diary for May 1915 records: "One can't help it—one cares no less for one's dog because there's a war. . . . I feel it [the dog's death] so terribly that my vitality seems squeezed out."[10] And yet, her strength restored, MDP returned to France both that fall and the next year to nurse during the especially terrible Battle of Verdun.[11] But for all her war efforts, she did not abandon her literary pursuits. In 1915 she published a controversial book of moral and theological reflections on war, *Reflections of a Non-Combatant*.

The book was not very clearly written. The main lines may have been obvious enough: societies should aim at "the transformation of the social and political and international conditions that render war inevitable."[12] Until national selfishness is curbed in the larger interests of humanity, war is inevitable and it is useless to pretend that it is a sport or played by polite rules. But should nations try to "civilize" warfare, mitigate its brutality by observing standards and rules? If Maude Petre thought this, she did not stress it in her book. An unsigned review in the *Catholic World* found her work tended to beget "a cynical acquiescence in . . . sad moral decadence."[13]

In reflecting back on the First World War in her autobiography, Maude Petre clarified some of her thought. In terms of "making war more civilized," for instance, she said that she had been asked whether it would not be better to trim the claws of a beast that one could not destroy. She replied: "Certainly, if we can, but better to let war show her own hideous reality than paint her up to look like a decent member of society." Also in her later writing, she rejected the idea that war was inevitable because humanity seemed to have an innate fighting instinct. War, she noted, is made "by force of mind."[14]

Maude Petre did not consider herself a pacifist, for she felt a responsibility to stand by the country on which she was dependent for life. But should the whole nation take a collective step in the direction of peace, she could then happily follow. Some may find a unilateral step toward peace a kind of madness, Petre realized; but she wondered whether such a step could be any madder than those steps that would lead to war.[15]

Twenty-two years later, before the outbreak of another World War, Maude Petre was to quote from her prophetic book of 1915. She had feared that during the period of reaction to the war seeds of lasting hatred would be sown. Those seeds, she cautioned, could "bring forth, perhaps in many years to come, a fresh outbreak of horrors we never witnessed unless all that is best in mankind be brought to the making of peace."[16] The most effective making of peace, the only "sound pacificism," MDP observed in her later meditation on the subject, was that which "develops the common interests as between States; which directs trade and commerce to union and not rivalry; which promotes intellectual intercourse in every way. . . ."[17]

One basic theme in MDP's writings throughout the war years was to the effect that human nature is redeemable but not yet redeemed, and so some moral compromise is inevitable. Religion may never simply deny fundamental drives and instincts, she wrote; "but on the other hand no religion is worth preserving unless its demands are higher than those of our actual existence."[18] But having made such an allowance, Maude Petre returned to that nationalistic special pleading that seemed to mark her thought and writing in this period. In words that sound strangely familiar to American ears of a later generation, she even declared at one point: "Be our country right or wrong, we must clear out of it or defend it."[19]

More intriguing from the point of view of the history of Modernism, though, was MDP's comparison of German absolutism in the war to the Vatican's absolutism under Pius X. To protest such German ultramontanism, she wrote, was the very purpose of the Allies under President Wilson's leadership. All those "principles of self-determination and liberty of free development and Progress" proclaimed by the Allies had their religious counterpart in the Modernist quest. When the Modernists had expressed such aspirations in terms of the historical and philosophical, it had seemed unreal and idealistic; it took the war to make more practically urgent those aspirations that many had considered vague.[20] Many people, Petre argued, had not a word of complaint against Rome when it dealt summarily with intellectual matters; but "they saw the mischief when their own national and patriotic ideals were involved."[21]

In 1918, the year that the Great War ended, Maude Petre published *Democracy at the Cross-Roads*. The title is reminiscent of Tyrrell's 1910 *Christianity at the Cross-Roads* and is probably meant by Maude to present the same kind of reorientation in the political and social fields that Tyrrell had offered in the more strictly theological. Perhaps more than in any of her other writings, Maude Petre gave evidence here of her aristocratic background. If social classes were to be dissolved in the postwar world, if noble classes were to fall before the onrush of democracy, then MDP was most anxious that the best of the virtues, values, and responsibilities of the nobility should pass to the people along with the privileges. Aristocratic upbringing, flawed though it may have been, "did often prepare men to take into consideration other interests than their own." Society should strive not just for more money and less work. The goal should not be just more materialistic abundance but a "nobler and more spiritual world."[22]

The fuller and selfless life, the attaining of a more deeply human quality of living that would inevitably be grounded on the transcendent—this would be a constant theme in the postwar writings of Maude Petre. This emphasis on the developed and deeper spiritual quality of life for all people in the world community would mean that her writings more and more were a blending of religious, social, and political areas of thought. As she herself admitted, the World War with its suffering and consequent upheavals in the social and political domains had caused her to deal with concepts "not professedly religious." And, she added, "for me, no subject that regards humanity can be without a leading religious signification."[23]

Democracy at the Cross-Roads provides a good exemplar of such a blending, for it announces that the goal of political, governmental, and industrial systems is to free all people to strive for the higher life. And the higher life and its relationship to religion is delineated in what might be called a Christian-humanist manifesto:

> Sport is more amusing, dancing is more delightful, music is more entrancing, poetry is more exalting, science is more engrossing, philosophy is more absorbing, love is worth all of them together and religion gives to the whole world that seal of eternity without which all human life, all human interests, all human efforts are but ripples on the ocean of immensity. Family life, artistic life, intellectual life, religious life—when all these flourish in a land the best ends of a government are attained.[24]

Democracy will most certainly have need of religion, Maude Petre maintained; but in her 1918 work she would not pursue the question of whether traditional Christianity would be most appropriate. She contented herself by saying that the spiritual ideals of democracy were such that could only exist at "a temperature which only religion can generate." A society lacking "other world and eternal ideals," prayers, sacraments, and enduring faith and hope, she said, could not ultimately survive.[25]

In 1919, Maude Petre collaborated with James A. Walker on a small volume, *State Morality and a League of Nations*. This study presented the differing views of Petre and James Walker on the role the state should assume in furthering human aspirations. Walker tended to look upon the state as a moral personality that could be possessed of Christian goals and actions. But Maude Petre looked for the advancement of human ideals less from the domain of political action than from the progress of humanity.[26]

She insisted that the duty of the state is primarily the preservation of the material rather than the moral welfare of its citizens. "The state will progress," she wrote, "as humanity progresses; it will have a more directly moral end as the people which compose it."[27]

MDP further held that international morality was in the process of development, but that it had by no means yet arrived. She thought it a "misdirection of energy to suppose moral excellences that are not in accordance with life as it now exists." And yet, though the world may not be ready for full international solidarity, MDP thought that a ". . . League of Nations signifies nothing at all unless it means a move in that direction." In addition to the League of Nations, she thought there should be established an International Council representing labor, capital, intellect, industry, religion, and many other fields.[28]

But if humanity is to come to a more ideal condition, political maneuvering alone will not suffice. Genuine human solidarity, Maude Petre wrote, can arise only on a religious base that constantly confronts humanity with belief in the ultimacy of a supreme good. And if spiritual ideals are to remain in the human line of vision, the churches as the vehicle of "corporate belief in spiritual ideals" will be required; individual spiritual insight alone could never perform such a collective task.[29]

The postwar years were, of course, a time of political and economic turmoil; a time of an ineffective League of Nations and of the rivalries of communism, fascism, and democracy. One great thinker who lived through these times—Teilhard de Chardin—regarded all three systems as partial attempts to achieve, from different emphases and angles, a totalization of humanity, an expression of individual integrity within a context of the corporateness of the human family.[30] Maude Petre had examined democracy in her 1918 study, and she would study communism in articles in the 1930s and 40s. In 1923 she translated and wrote an introduc-

tion to a book by Pietro Gorgolini.[31] The English edition of this
book, *The Fascist Movement in Italian Life*, had a short preface by
Benito Mussolini.

In her introduction, Maude Petre discussed Italian political
types, among them, Machiavelli and Mazzini.[32] Too often MDP
thought, Machiavelli's positive contributions had been forgotten.
He had, after all, urged citizens to avoid rivalry and seek public
good over private pleasure.[33]

One of Maude Petre's more concise statements of humanity's deeper needs was in another short book she published in
1925, entitled *The Two Cities*. Once again, familiar themes are
sounded: the world must beware of those who "claimed to represent the weak, but only until they themselves become strong"; a
"poison of egotism" has always infected past attempts at the better-
ment of the world.[34] But a heightened intensity came into the proceedings when Maude Petre turned to the relationship of a developed humanity and religious faith.

MDP observed that she did not seek to prove to anyone the
existence of God. Echoing Pascal, she noted that those who
sought God had already "in some measure found Him." But if she
would not seek to prove God's existence, Petre did pose a question: "whether, in fact . . . brotherly love has ever maintained
itself on its own resources." Faith is a requisite of any great human
undertaking, but faith in humanity alone always proves inadequate.[35] It is clearly implicit in this line of reasoning that the at-
tainment of any genuine human solidarity depends on the grounding of the human in the divine.

The faith needed by a regenerated humanity must be a most
embracing one: It must not only lend meaning and zest to life, but
a dignity and comfort to death as well, since the corporate structure of the world will perish as surely as the individual within it.
The human assurance must be that "the vicissitudes of this little
planet are the object of a vast solicitude."[36] This solicitude of God
for men and women becomes most apparent in an incarnational
perspective, and Maude Petre explicitly spoke in such terms:

> Put in God and humanity becomes Divine—worthy of that heroic
> effort and self-abandonment by which alone we achieve social
> regeneration. Put in Christ, and God becomes Human, near
> enough, like enough, to guide and support our efforts.[37]

And so humanity longs for a regenerated world, yet is seemingly locked in this "terribly bad one." If religion has failed in bringing people from the old to the new, is the world to be without hope? On the contrary, religion has the greater task now before it. Believers must act to better the present world—an imperative often neglected in a perspective that could become exclusively other-worldly. Maude Petre held for the interpenetration of this world and the next.[38]

"Religion," MDP wrote, "is wider than the Churches which preach it." It is, of course, the Christian religion that is inevitably woven into Western society. "It may be that both are to go: but the civilization will not remain without the religion, even if the religion should remain without the civilization."[39] But religion itself is vital and urgently needed for the spiritual growth of humanity and Petre reiterated her religio-humanist perspective:

> to seek the City of God is veritably to seek the City of Humanity—for whatever is for the good of man, of all man, and of all men, of man both soul and body, both mind and matter, both angel and beast, is also, inevitably, for the honour and glory of God as well.[40]

In taking up the question of religion and bolshevism in her writings, Maude Petre examined that system that professed to seek the City of Humanity without reference to the City of God. She spoke of bolshevism as a rival religion in a 1932 article, noting that bolshevism possessed three requisites of all religion: worship, sacrifice, and service.[41] Only, the Bolshevist professes to substitute collective humanity for an outworn God. Almost a decade later, in an essay entitled "What Russia Can Teach Us," Maude Petre noted that the democracies had much to learn from the Bolshevist-Communist history of Russia: Often individuals had rested content in economic security for themselves, unmindful of desperate social needs. Such greediness can lead men and women to correspondingly desperate attempts at redress—to sacrifice liberty to the ambition of the State.[42]

Religion, too, may have failed in calling humanity to a proper social concern. But the Christian message remains one "of sharing, of human equality, of the rights of powerful and humble alike." Christianity, however, "now seems to fear its own primitive

ideal" as communism professes it; but that is because communism
has given in to violence as a means of persuasion and has failed
to accord each individual personal respect. But it is possible,
Maude Petre insisted, to decry the vice of bolshevism while continuing to respect communism. In fact, she wrote, her dream for
the postwar world was "the reconciliation of Christianity and
Communism:"

> The Christian and the Communist have torn each other in the
> dark because they could not see that human society needed them
> both: that true Communism was the earthly complement of Chris-
> tianity—while Christianity was the spiritual complement of Com-
> munism. . . . I do not believe that Communism can ultimately sur-
> vive divorced from Christianity.[43]

And while democracy and communism may be teaching each
other lessons, Christianity has a lesson for both:

> human nature as we know it, is not wholly perfectible . . . our
> ideal society—call it communistic or socialistic or Democratic, or
> what you will—cannot be brought on earth save by a long process
> of discipline and self-sacrifice; . . . some compulsion may have to
> be exercised but the true motive power can only be love.[44]

After observing for two decades the attempts of communism, democracy and fascism to structure viable societies, Maude
Petre contributed a suggestion of her own in 1939. Entitled
"Nationalism and Christianity: Can Christianity Save the World?"
it appeared as a supplement to *Adelphi* magazine in July 1939—
ironically enough, two months before the start of the Second
World War.[45]

The past had seen flawed attempts at the reordering of the
world that had miserably failed; most noticeable in modern times
had been the League of Nations. This last had a real opportunity
of bringing a Christian ethic to bear on international life, but it
failed because "it was mainly a parliament of nations and not of
mankind, and each member had to present the interests of his
own country, not those of all mankind."[46] To remedy this failure,
Maude Petre suggested the general lines of a new "Society of
Nations" whose members would represent human, not merely
national, needs. This society would have for its working principle
the Beatitudes of Jesus.

Petre examined each Beatitude for its possible application in world affairs. Nations must become, for example, poor in spirit if wars are to be avoided and the quality of human life deepened. That is to say, nations will still need to own and possess, but they must begin to "regard their possessions as a trust, to be exercised for the good of others as much as themselves."[47] Meekness, ability to admit error, would also be necessary if nations are to prevent future conflict.[48] In such a manner MDP traced through all the Beatitudes.

After pointing out that her proposed society would meet under the leadership of people working for love rather than money and in an assembly hall that would exemplify the spirit of poverty, Maude Petre returned to her central theme: that such a project would be unworkable without Christianity. Why was Christianity so uniquely fitted to such a task?

> Christianity has a message for all humanity, and a message for both time and eternity. Do we live in past, or present, or future, or do we live in the lasting reality which underlies them all? This sense of lastingness is not just an element of the Christian faith; it is the deepest consciousness of the human soul, and only unnoticed because it is deeper than any other consciousness.[49]

The sense of the lasting eternal value of all men and women —coupled with an awareness of their ongoing deeply human needs had driven Maude Petre on in these years between the wars to search out the basis for workable national and world governments, based on fundamentally Christian principles. But for all her political and social concern, she did not neglect more specifically religious concepts and institutions. And she continued to meditate upon the worth of Modernism in her later years.

8

Modernism's Early Historian

IN 1918 MAUDE PETRE moved from being a participant caught up in the storms of Modernism to being one of the first historians and analysts of the movement. In that year of the Great War's conclusion, she published *Modernism: Its Failures and Its Fruits*, dedicating it to George Tyrrell with the observation "that life may be well spent in sowing what we shall not reap and that it is enough to see the Promised Land from afar though it be not given us to enter therein."[1]

By way of definition, Petre spoke of the Modernist as one who believes in the "possibility of a synthesis between the essential truth of his religion and the essential truth of modernity."[2] A proper reading of Modernism, in fact, presented the sensitive thinker with a series of paradoxes:

> Modernism is a movement in the Church, but not a Church movement. . . . It is a religious movement, yet the official representatives of religion repudiate it; it is a deeply human movement, yet the larger section of humanity cares nothing for it. It is a learned movement, yet learning regards it more frequently with pity than with respect; it is an unlearned movement, yet the simple and unlearned look on it with fear and suspicion rather than love.[3]

And if the official Church was the constant critic of Modernism, MDP was quite sure she knew why: the Church had overreached itself. The Church had erred for centuries, she wrote, by "regarding religion as her own peculiar possession." Religion, "which is universal as humanity itself," need not depend solely on the Church; the Church should be a means to religious experience, not an end in itself. Modernism, in Maude Petre's reading of it, tried "to make religion paramount and the Church secondary; to restore the Church to her position of guardian, but not mistress, of religious faith and life."[4]

Having made her own position relatively clear, she employed it in yet one further attempt at definition.

> [Modernism] is, in fact, one of two things. It is either the last explosive movement of vitality in institutions doomed to proximate extinction, at least in so far as they can be considered of worldwide importance, or it is the beginning of a new condition of things, in which the church shall be subservient to the religious and spiritual needs of humanity; shall preserve the truth committed to her guardianship, but shall not refuse to learn that which mankind can teach her; shall guide and command, but also follow and obey.[5]

Significantly, as her analysis continued, Maude Petre introduced an argument not generally heard in the early accounts of Modernism: it was not so much an intellectual's aberration as a pastoral response to a widely felt human need. Tyrrell had repeatedly met people in counseling who were crushed in spirit by dry and overly analytical scholastic theology. Loisy too could be said to be ministering to the "unconscious Modernism" of the many who tried to make sense of the Scriptures in the modern era.[6]

Maude Petre's sense of the importance of the laity in Catholicism would be an underlying current throughout her study. Perhaps with an eye on Newman's great stand for the *sensus fidelium*, MDP judged that the Church is alive and full of spiritual need and insight in its lay people, even if the authority of that Church fails to respond accordingly. She listed a catalogue of the maladies—in addition to the challenges of modern science—that affected the simple believer before "conscious Modernism" attempted a response:

> he suffered . . . from the subtleties of theology, which disturbed his devotional life; from the literal and unspiritual interpretation of Scripture, which shocked his moral sense; from the encouragement of low and material forms of devotion, which weakened his spiritual life; from a system of education, and a general treatment of faith difficulties, which exposed him, sooner or later, to the ruin of his faith.[7]

In her exposition of conscious Modernism, Maude Petre considered the relationship of faith to four categories: philosophy, history, theology, and social ideals. The first section, that on philosophy and faith, examined the orientation of such men as Blondel, Laberthonnière, and LeRoy and their conviction that faith signifies far more than intellectual acceptance of formula; rather, faith must bespeak the response of the whole human complexity—mind, will, emotions—to the call of God's word. Or, as Petre encapsulated this orientation, "faith demands, not only mental docility, but moral self-donation."[8]

Here, then, was but one example of the new apologetic approach that Maude Petre saw underlying Modernism. But she was not in perfect agreement with proponents of this apologetic. She feared that Blondel, for instance, did not carry his logic far enough, and did not sufficiently realize the possibility of conflict of science and/or history with metaphysics. By objecting too sternly to a rigid distinction of sciences, these new philosophers refused to each domain its "legitimate autonomy."[9] Thus, when Laberthonnière underplayed historical problems about Jesus by insisting on his ongoing presence in the world, MDP objected:

> we feel that two orders of knowledge are being inadequately distinguished; that, unless we may depend on the brutal historical value of certain facts, Jesus of Nazareth cannot be for us 'the way, the truth, and the life.' We need not personally verify all those facts, yet confidence we do require in their actual historic happening.[10]

Granted that history might not prove the "spiritual signification of a fact," she said, still the men in question were "wrong when they restricted history in its dealing with the fact itself."[11]

The second section, on history and faith, developed these historical problems somewhat by examining Loisy's thought on the question. Loisy stressed history's autonomy, and working on his historical principles and researches in Scripture, he developed conclusions that had proved upsetting: Jesus did not historically found the Church, "nor did He teach the Catholic doctrine as to His own Divinity." If Loisy had stopped at his criticisms, Maude Petre observed, he would not really be a Modernist; rather it was his attempt to maintain the truths of revelation in the face of the criticism that qualified him for the Modernist designation.[12] From Loisy's approach, two facts are "established for all time," MDP thought, that the Christian religion in history "is marked by strong and persistent vitality" and its "inner meaning is no way disproved by . . . criticism"; and that no religion can "touch . . . use . . . or depend on history, without, in so far, becoming subject to the laws of history."[13]

The examination of the third area, theology and faith, not surprisingly, is built around Tyrrell's thought. Once again, familiar themes appear: theology is dependent on spiritual and devotional life rather than vice-versa; people must depend on revelation in their spiritual lives, but that revelation should be considered in terms of an "infusion of divine experience" and not just of theological formulations.[14] MDP quoted from one of Tyrrell's unpublished essays, "Revelation and Experience," to point out that Christ is truly God's fullest revelation to the world. Yet, the records of that revelation preserve "not the theology, but the spirit of Christ. Hence those records have an absolute and abiding value as the history of a supreme divine experience, while the dogmas in which they are encrusted have but a relative one."[15] Tyrrell's attempt, then, was described as an attempt to preserve the realities behind the theological language, so that those realities could survive even the most devastating assault on their theological formulations.[16]

While she was immersed in George Tyrrell's thought in this section of her study of Modernism, Maude Petre helpfully provided her own catalogue of what she considered the most important characteristics of her friend's thought:

1. "a very strong sense of the transcendental character of religion;"
2. "a definitely Catholic, as opposed to an individualistic, outlook;"
3. "as in the 'Philosophy of action,' a firmly anti-intellectualist temper;"
4. "a full, at times almost too full, recognition of the part played by the will in an act of faith;"
5. "a deep sense of the supremacy of conscience and of the sense of righteousness, as the basis of religion;"
6. "a profound spirit of mysticism;"
7. "a perception of the need and rights of the ordinary mind, and

of the duty of religious teachers to minister to those needs and respect those rights."[17]

The last of the four sections dealing with conscious Modernism concerned social ideals and faith and made reference to the Italian Modernist priest-leader Romolo Murri and the French layman Marc Sangnier. From the Modernist perspective, Maude Petre insisted, the central question was not whether democracy or socialism were the better form of government; rather the Modernist would ask "whether democracy and Socialism could find a place in the Church" or were the traditional authoritarian forms considered "essential to her own existence?" The social Modernists, of course, held that the Church should display more sympathy for democracy and also championed more lay action within the Church. The official answer of the Church, MDP noted, as given by Pope Pius X, was disappointing to the Modernist aspirations. Pope Pius had spoken of the God-established orders and levels in human society and considered lay action independent of Church authority to be illegitimate.[18] For all her own personal interest in the social questions, though, Maude Petre still maintained that a pivotal problem of Modernism was that of the relation of theology to history. More specifically, the crisis arose over questions of Christology.[19]

What specifically, are some of these christological problems? MDP mentioned four: the historicity of the Resurrection; Christ's affirmation of his own divinity; the knowledge of Jesus; and the foundation of the Church, hierarchy, and sacraments by Christ directly. Noting that the impregnability of Loisy's position on these problems was "a matter beyond the judgment of the present writer," Petre nevertheless presented Loisy's thinking on the disputed points.[20] On the Resurrection, the French critic had thought no "indisputable argument" could be drawn in its favor, for the "risen Christ belongs no more to the order of present life"; at best, the New Testament evidence offers only "a limited probability."[21] Loisy considered that the historical Jesus neither taught his own divinity nor directly established a Church hierarchy or sacraments.[22] As to the infallible knowledge of Jesus, Loisy considered that "the critic only knows this thesis in the history of theology."[23]

Maude Petre observed that, though the "leading facts" of Jesus' life had come to be known even more certainly than they were before criticism, yet people were deeply disturbed by the threat of future critical findings.[24] Several theories had been advanced to meet such a situation: the distinction of the Eternal Christ from the Jesus of history, the seeking in Christ of a mere "unique manifestation of the love of God and the love of man," or the eschatological approach that takes the "hard sayings" of Jesus about the coming judgment without the intervening layers of interpretations. No final solution to such perplexities in Christology was yet forthcoming, Maude Petre indicated.[25]

Reflecting on problems such as that posed by the christological question, Maude Petre spoke of the need for Christianity to undergo a "transformation . . . of a very fundamental nature."[26] Secular society had to adjust to a Copernican revolution; Christianity must now make a similar adjustment:

> We have not, eventually, found the world any smaller because it forms part of a larger system; Christianity will not prove less important because it is not only *religion* but also a *religion*. . . . [27]

In Jesus, MDP insisted, humanity finds "the primary, classic and supreme revelation" of God, and criticism can never interfere with such a judgment. But in keeping with her call for a religious Copernican revolution, she saw a special problem in traditional Christology.

> Our difficulties begin when Jesus Christ must not only be to us the chief manifestation of the Divinity, but must be it in such a way that those who are without Him are without any such revelation. The mystical Christ of the Church is God, and God belongs to all men, and is revealed in a greater or less degree in every religion.[28]

Still, any religion, to be considered genuinely Christian, must possess the "person . . . history . . . and the worship of Christ."[29] So that, for Maude Petre, should Christ cease to be "in some sense, our teacher, our Master and our God," Christianity would be drained of its religious meaning.[30] MDP's christological conclusions undoubtedly seemed more radical to her contemporaries than they would to later theological generations. She held to the divinity of Jesus as the Christ while also holding that revelation was not confined to the person of Christ.

Maude Petre followed up her discussion of the specific substantive problems of history and Christology by examining the relationship of Modernism and the organized structures of the churches. Why has Modernism attained such force precisely in the Roman communion? Dean William Inge (1860–1954) of St. Paul's Cathedral had considered it "preposterous" that Modernism should arise in a Church so attached to authoritarianism as Rome.[31] But, Petre noted, Modernism raised questions vital to *all* Christian churches. It so happens that the questioning is more acute in Catholicism, since Protestantism, not having a centralized head, "is not always aware of the vital changes it is undergoing." In Catholicism "with a single brain, wherever that brain may be situated," the "crises assume at once an universal character."[32] Why would Modernists remain in the Roman Church that so opposed the movement? Maude Petre responded that the Catholic Church introduced the dimension of healthy tension within one's religious life:

> When there is no positive external restraint on our professions and opinions we may, with an agreeable, but inexact vagueness, wander a good way from our post, and think we are still beside it.[33]

In a chapter called "The Official Church and Modernism," MDP continued her examination of the relationship of the new religious movement and institutional religion. In particular, she traced out reactions to the papal documents of 1907. The decree *Lamentabili* was adjudged "extraordinarily elusive," while both the decree and the encyclical *Pascendi* are said to "fail conspicuously in giving a fair account of the writings to which they tacitly refer."[34] But the Church was not completely unjust in her condemnation:

> For it is, indeed, at the very foundations of faith that modernism has expended its labours, just as it is at the very foundations of human science and truth that the engines of the Church are directed in its condemnation.[35]

The Church saw clearly the force of the new religious approaches; but to have expected the Church to be agreeable to the Modernist movement would be to ask of that same Church "a line of conduct surpassing the elevation and force of the human elements of which she is composed." The Church, after all, had a long history that would make the Modernist stance unacceptable.[36]

The "root problem of the whole modernist controversy," Maude Petre finally judged, was the question of the limits of authority within the Church.[37] In fact, she thought that if the authority problem had been raised on its own before the Modernist movement began, the course of the conflict might have been very different.[38] The authority question affected all the other areas in which the Modernists were concerned: science, history, theology, and philosophy. Modernists in all these areas agreed in "not denying the essential need of some form of authority, but insisting on its limits."[39] The Modernist, she said, *does* want "to obey the Pope, but to obey him in just measure"; it is not the Pope's power but its exaggeration that caused a crisis.[40]

Significantly, writing in 1918, Maude Petre finds "a certain sympathy" between representatives of excessive papal authoritarianism and autocractic militarism.[41] In later years she would insist further that Modernism was a religious movement whose aims were akin to those of the Allies in the First World War:

> Modernism was . . . deeply representative of the aims of the world war; that its leaders were men inspired, in religious questions, with the same ideals as those for which we were fighting in national life; that it was, in fact, a spiritual struggle for the principle of rightful liberty and self-determination. The aim of its leaders was to make the Church "safe for democracy"; to bring the mechanism of religious life into accordance with the free spontaneous life of heart and head in the believer.[42]

By what standard, then, does the individual Catholic justify obedience at all, if it is to be a limited or conditional obedience? It was, after all, a problem with which MDP was most personally acquainted. She developed her own position in terms of the wider community will:

> The object of religious obedience is to unite us with one another, and to unite us all, individually and collectively, with the Divine Will. Hence its aim is the destruction of self-seeking and self-interest, and the absorption of our narrower life into a wider and more universal one. . . . That authority should demand the sacrifice of our private interest is of the very reason for its existence; that it should demand the sacrifice of our universal interests is to contradict every motive for obedience.[43]

And concerning the papacy in particular, MDP was to write to Loisy her expectations for a greatly changed future:

> for me the Church's outer constitution is totally unimportant—it is, as you say, only the spirit that will survive. I know not if the Pope will hold a position in the coming religion, and I care not—all I do know and care about is his position and action, if he remains, should be deeply other than they are now. I do feel I believe with you that we are moving to a new religion—but I think that nothing dies and that Christiantiy will be a great, if not the greatest element in it. . . . [44]

As a test of limited obedience to the Church, at the end of her work Maude Petre turned to a consideration of resistance to the anti-Modernist oath of 1910. In the first place, MDP thought that the implication of requiring all ecclesiastics other than the Pope to take the oath was that "the Pope was not a heretic, but all the rest of the Church might be."[45] Apart from this general objection, she said that many a good Catholic would readily declare acceptance of infallible truths of the Church, as the oath required; however, the overall problem, as she had insisted in her dispute with Bishop Amigo,[46] was in the understanding of the range of infallibility.

On specific difficulties in the oath, MDP pointed to the assertion that God could be known with certainty by reason through causality and retorted that "the whole spirit of this assertion is contrary to that philosophy which would seek God inwardly. . . ."[47] She also noted that references to miracles as "very certain signs of the divine origin" of Christianity and to the Church as being directly instituted by the historical Jesus were disturbing.[48] In the oath's rejection of the evolution of dogmas such that they are different from the sense first assigned them by the Church, MDP saw "an assertion that is actually contrary to every theory of vital and organic development."[49]

The oath called for a profession that faith be accepted as "a true assent of the intelligence to truth acquired from outside." Maude Petre thought that such a "purely intellectualist view of faith" made discourse with agnostics and skeptics an impossibility. Finally, the declaration of the oath that condemned those who held that scholars must be free "from all preconceived opinions as to the supernatural origin of Catholic tradition" drew Petre's ire: "Here it is a question of whether history is to be pure history, or history controlled by theology."[50]

In a significant closing chapter of her history of Modernism, Maude Petre asked the vital questions as to whether Modernism had died the death and been "the last explosive movement of vitality" or if it were to be, in the words of the introductory chapter, "the beginning of a new condition of things."[51]

Actually, Maude Petre considered that the vital question was not whether Modernism would survive, but if, in fact, Catholicism would. Modernism would eventually pass away as a mere period piece that championed certain important notions in a unique historical situation of exploding knowledge. Against this background, Modernism made a certain demand:

> that religious faith must not only tolerate the co-existence of independent scientific, or historic, or philosophic truth, but must allow the play of such truth on her own domain wherever its rays can penetrate.[52]

Catholicism, however, would endure; yet she must not "subsist in virtue of her rejection of any form of truth."[53] When the Modernists had tried to formulate a new apologetical response to the skeptics and critics of Catholicism, Maude Petre said, the Church had condemned them, yet without providing answers to the questions they posed. This would only emphasize Petre's charge that the sin of pride in the Church "has closed [the Church's] heart to some of the legitimate needs and aspirations of humanity."[54]

If there be need for reform in the Church, there are various levels of attaining the goal—some more, some less radical. But, Maude Petre insisted, a radical change is needed in the under-

standing of faith. Faith cannot be seen as a "completeness of understanding of the religious truths"; in fact, although Modernists
were charged with immanentism for holding more to mystery
than to precision in faith, they showed themselves more properly
transcendental in orientation than their critics.[55] "In the face of intellectual difficulties," MDP wrote, "there are two conceptions of
faith." According to the one approach, men believe in spite of contrary evidence; while according to the second, "we maintain our
religious faith as something that lies beyond the reach of those difficulties." Roughly speaking, one may attribute to anti-Modernists
the former position, and to Modernists the latter.[56] This sense of
incompleteness may discourage the more traditional; but it is a
fact of life for moderns. It is a natural enough human trait to
seek a narrow precision and completeness; but the "passage from
this exclusiveness to a wider life" is a necessary transformation
through which individuals and societies must go if they are to
grow strong.[57]

What, finally, does the Modernist profess as faith? Does the
emphasis on incompleteness cause Modernist believers to throw
up their hands in a hopeless vagueness? In concluding her study
of Modernism, Maude Petre attempted a fairly lengthy Modernist
Credo which would undoubtedly surprise many critics because it
had a certain kind of orthodox fullness all its own. Surely a fitting
conclusion to the study of Maude Petre's 1918 work *Modernism:
Its Failure and Its Fruits* would be an abridged version of her own
Modernist credo:

> Religion is [for the Modernist] the supreme interest in life; but it
> cannot be lived alone, and he needs a Church . . . adapted to the
> needs of all. . . . Neither Church nor State can exist without some
> principle of unity; hence he believes in authority, and accepts the
> existing ecclesiastical hierarchy. . . .
>
> He believes in Christianity as the highest form of religion
> which man has attained; he worships Christ as God; and he
> believes that, in the historic Christ, the Divinity was manifested.
> He believes that God reveals Himself to man in diverse manners;
> he believes in the sacramental system . . . in prayer . . . in
> sacrifice . . . in obedience to rightful authority . . . in the humble,
> daily practices of Catholic life.

On the other hand, he does not believe in the Church as an end, but as a means. . . . Living within her he accepts her doctrines, her customs, her regulations, in the same way as he accepts the Church herself—that is to say, relatively to that wider life for which she exists. . . .

He does not believe that Jesus Christ, as known to history, can be known otherwise than by historical methods. . . .

He does not believe that any of the doctrines or practices of the Catholic life have been exhaustively comprehended, or finally explained. . . .

He believes, lastly, that he has a place in the Church, because he maintains that it is the Church's own life that is stirring within him . . . as contained in no fixed form or quantity, but as the outpouring of infinity.[58]

While it may legitimately be doubted that such a Modernist as Alfred Loisy would sign such a declaration, it is clear that Maude Petre would have solemnly affixed her signature to this creed. Together with Maude's declaration of reasons for remaining in the Catholic Church contained in her 1937 autobiography, *My Way of Faith*, this credo offers the most mature, concise, and developed statement of Maude Petre's understanding of her own Modernism.

9

"After All Our Hopes":

THE LATER YEARS

AFTER THE YEARS OF the Modernist crisis and the World War, Maude Petre's life settled into quieter, less dramatic ways. Although she traveled a bit, such as her trip to South Africa in 1926, in her sixties and seventies she was leading largely a literary life. After the history of Modernism in 1918, she produced such books as *The Two Cities* (1925), *The Ninth Lord Petre* (1928), *My Way of Faith* (1937), *Von Hügel and Tyrrell: The Story of a Friendship* (1937), and *Alfred Loisy: His Religious Significance* (published posthumously, in 1944) and nearly fifty periodical articles.

In the years between the World Wars, two theological themes continued to figure prominently in Maude Petre's writings. This chapter will consider each of these in its turn: (1) an ongoing analysis of Modernism and its adherents and (2) the nature of the Church. A third section will deal with the last days and death of Maude Petre.

For the most part, MDP had made her own nearly definitive analysis of Modernism in *Modernism: Its Failures and Its Fruits*. And yet, she continued to bring greater precision to this account in her later writings. By 1937, for example, in *My Way of Faith*, MDP listed six reasons the institutional church opposed Modernism:

(1) [Modernism] impugned the intellectual certainty of dogma and doctrine, or, rather, its intellectual *convincingness*. The Church . . . had no place for the honest doubter.
(2) It accepted historical evidence, even when such evidence ran counter to the traditional presentment of revealed truth.
(3) It found religious truth elsewhere, as well as in the Church.

(4) It appeared to under-rate the letter to the benefit of the spirit.

(5) It introduced a note of relativity in the conception of theology and dogma.

(6) It admitted of a democratic ideal of social life; such an ideal as might affect hierarchical values in both State and Church.

Over against these reasons for which the Church rejected the Modernist movement, Maude Petre offered the pleas the Modernists would make against *Pascendi*: (1) grave problems did face the traditional Church teaching, no matter how much authority might try to ignore them; (2) some might be untroubled by new thought currents, but many minds were honestly troubled; (3) faith could survive the present challenge; (4) the Modernists—at least the ones MDP knew personally—"had no overweening belief in the finality of human knowledge, but neither could they discount it;" (5) the Church cannot behave as if she were immune from the problems facing all men; (6) the Church showed signs of "worldliness;" if she were more spiritual, she could "triumph over difficulties that were fatal to a more rationalistic conception of her authority and teaching."[1]

The later years, in fact, brought Maude Petre to a more expansive, though more critical view of the movement in which she had so deeply immersed herself. By 1933 she had told Loisy's friend Louis Canet that "the old disputes within the Church are to some extent, unimportant now—there are bigger issues—if the Church can uphold spiritual values, that is all that matters."[2] In a very significant admission of 1937, she spoke of the necessity and rights of orthodoxy. "If the Church be a city on earth," she wrote, "orthodoxy is the cement that has been employed in her walls and buildings."[3] She even went so far as to admit the "inevitability of certain disciplinary acts" within Catholicism because "the Church is a Church of the present and not of the future":

> [The Church] is capable, if true to her mission, of indefinite growth and expansion; but actually she cannot go beyond the stage which she has reached. Officially, like all state authority, she must lag behind even the best of her own people; and she is bound, like every wise government, to seek "safety first."[4]

MDP had mellowed, but not very much. She was to remain a consistently loyal critic of Catholicism. Because the Church had been supreme teacher so long, Maude Petre said laconically, "she forgot that she must also be the supreme learner."[5]

In the 1920s and 1930s, MDP also showed further insight into particular leaders in the Modernist movement. Von Hügel, for instance, she never quite forgave for having introduced Tyrrell to critical Scripture studies without an assurance that he could deal properly with them.[6] She suspected that the Baron was actually relieved when Tyrrell died; and though von Hügel attended the funeral, she thought he would have been "glad not to attend."[7] Furthermore, the Baron was said to have an obsession that theologians were becoming immanentists.[8]

While maintaining sympathy for Loisy in these later years, Petre took him to task for his humanism, which she thought lacked a fundamental grounding in spiritual reality. Looking to the Frenchman's demand for unconditional faith in human nature, MDP reminded her readers that human faith, hope, and love "must have direct reference to that something greater than Humanity which alone justifies the existence of Humanity."[9] She objected, secondly, that Loisy's concept of revelation was deficient. Ultimately, she thought, revelation is "the belief that somehow comes to us and is not made by us; that it is the work of God on man, and not wholly the production of man himself."[10] Third, Maude Petre judged Loisy's humanism vitiated because it failed to satisfy the primal human need for prayer.[11] Finally, Loisy's religion of humanity looked almost entirely to the past for its models, heroes, and heroines. Christian liturgy is superior to Loisy's "worship" because:

> The dead live on, not only in the race, not only in our affections, but with a life of their own, whatever that life may be. As to Christ, would His memory have lasted so long had He only been a memory, and not, to faith, a living Reality?[12]

In short, while she considered Loisy to be reaching toward transcendence and deeper spirituality, she criticized him roundly for reducing faith to symbol alone. Even Pius X himself might have written (though it would have been with a more inflamed rhetoric) Maude Petre's rejection of some of the leaders of the "new humanism": "A method of sheer symbolism is no true method of faith . . . a fact which is resolved into nothing but a symbol loses its spiritual significance along with its material actuality."[13]

But one Frenchman appeared on the scene in these years between the wars in whom Maude Petre placed great confidence: Teilhard de Chardin. In her diary for 1938, MDP noted: "I have one great gain—to know the works of Père Teilhard de Chardin—a real revelation—and so much that I have said in my own way."[14] Dr. Alec Vidler, historian of Modernism and thoughtful observer of the modern theological scene, noted that he probably had heard the name of Teilhard for the first time from Maude Petre herself around 1940. Vidler wrote: "[Maude Petre] considered Teilhard de Chardin was attempting to do what the Roman Catholic Modernists would have done if they had been permitted to do their work."[15]

For MDP, both Loisy and Teilhard "sought in the history of earth and of humanity the message of hope and spiritual progress."[16] But Teilhard apparently satisfied her much more as being in closer touch with Christian orthodoxy. Her personal relations with the Jesuit Teilhard were not as satisfying, however. Her diary for September 13, 1938 points to great expectations: "Have had letter from P. Teilhard. I think something will be done between us—strange that a futurist told me that I should have a companionship for the end of my life." But the entry for August 1, 1939 is more somber. Regarding Teilhard, she writes only "had been a little disappointed in . . . personal relations with him." His name is not mentioned again.

These were not only the years of the rise of Teilhard de Chardin; they also saw the dominance of Neo-Orthodoxy in Protestantism. Maude Petre spoke favorably of this type of theology while allowing that "it has undoubtedly its way yet to go."[17] She described Karl Barth as one of the "men who have faced criticism in its fullest and most devastating force." "They have not refused the lesson of history," she wrote, "but they have somehow looked through history."[18] Even with reference to Neo-Orthodoxy, MDP found the work of Modernism helpful. Because Scripture scholars like Loisy had widened the very meaning of orthodoxy, Maude suggested, the Neo-Orthodox theologians had an easier go of it.[19]

Not surprisingly, as Maude Petre cast a slightly more critical eye over the Modernists during those twenty years which Robert Graves so aptly described as "the long weekend,"[20] she saved the greatest benefit of the doubt for her dear personal friend George Tyrrell. Had he lived longer, MDP broadly hints, Tyrrell would

have held to the fundamental faith while awaiting the "still far dis-
tant ideal of a truly Catholic religion."[21] After all, the English
Jesuit had considered Catholicism "the oldest and widest body of
corporate Christian experience" and "the closest approximation so
far attained to the Catholic ideal."[22] MDP seemed to feel that Tyrrell's thought would have widened out somewhat like her own.
His Modernism, she always insisted, was deeply interwound with
a Catholic conception of life:

> Some will ask what, then, he meant by that Modernism to which
> he adhered. He meant, by it, a belief in the religious needs of man-
> kind and in the inherent power of the Catholic Church to satisfy
> those needs. . . . He had entered the Church to work for others
> and not for himself; he asked for nothing, and he got nothing, but
> the exile's grave, with the symbol of priesthood over his head.[23]

One last personal point with regard to Tyrrell. Maude Petre
never became completely unobjective or uncritical about her
old friend. In the last article published before her death, MDP
was capable of saying that "Tyrrell was plain, not to say ugly in
appearance."[24]

As is now evident from even the partial inventory of her
writings that this study has provided, Maude Dominica Petre
focused her theological themes around the nature of the Church
itself; that is to say, she was an ecclesiologist.

She frequently faced the question of whether there was still
even a need for the Church in the modern situation. "Just because
there are so many possible roads through time to eternity, do we
need to choose one road; just because of the vastness of life, do
we need a shelter."[25] In an open letter to Lord Halifax in the summer of 1923, MDP called the Church "our home . . . our ark on
the immeasured waters." "We know that we know but little, but
we trust that the spiritual goods set before us are a pledge of those
that are to be."[26] Later that same fall, writing in the *Modern
Churchman*, she returned to the theme of the Church as a haven
from the immensity of the universe. Against the despair that often
flows from such immensity, the Church offers a human home
with a roof neither too high nor too low. "To live under a low
ceiling is oppressive; to live under too high a ceiling is to live under
no ceiling at all."[27]

In many ways, Petre's approach to the nature and necessity of the Church were rather traditional. The Church is said to be "the custodian of an eternal message, the historian . . . of the manifestation of God in humanity."[28] Religion remains "dim, vague, undefined and often impotent," until it has assumed "definite form and a concrete organization."[29]

Ecclesiastical authority was at least partly correct during the Modernist battles, MDP later allowed, since doctrinal development cannot be carried out "in obedience to history and science alone; it must respond to religious needs also."[30] And so the Church was seen as the guardian of the devotional life and needs of the human family. Most especially, the particular strength of the Roman Catholic Church was to be found, Petre maintained, in its stress on the Real Presence in the Eucharist and the Real Divinity in Christology.[31]

But never let it be said that with all her appreciation of the Catholic Church, Maude Petre did not remain as well its determined critic. Her works are never shy on catalogues of evils in the Church. Catholicism was beset, she thought, with "untruthfulness, domination, avarice and sloth."[32] In another place she remonstrated against the Church's "anti-democratic temper . . . its reprobation of Socialism, the position of the pope in relation to bishops and faithful" and its "doctrine of exclusiveness— extra Ecclesiam nulla salus".[33] Maude also continued to the end of her days to battle theologically against the possibility of an unending hell, an idea she thought the Church had overstressed for many centuries.[34]

Petre's critique of Catholicism took special focus in many of her late comments on the Modernist movement. Too often, she wrote, "Rome lauds and trusts those who are submissive because they do not care, and blames and mistrusts those who resist her because they do care."[35] The papacy had overreached itself by yielding to the ultramontane spirit.

By contrast, the old English Cisalpines with whom MDP identified herself and her family,[36] had allowed the papacy an honest but reverent regard because they believed "the thing itself was holy and essential in spite of its vices and faults."[37] And, one of the worst charges of all, MDP suggested that the Church had lost its nerve, had lost faith in itself during the Modernist crisis. Pope Pius X had spoken of Modernism as striking at the root of

Christian belief. Rather, Maude thought, the divine truth was "greater and more all-embracing than any merely human discovery." In short, "the roots must meet deeper down than any axe can reach."[38]

Fortunately, against the background of so many diverse statements, MDP left behind her a short summary of her faith in the Church, her Catholic apologia. Many had written books to say why they entered the Church of Rome; others wrote to explain why they left. Maude Petre wrote *My Way of Faith* to indicate why she remained in the Roman Catholic Church—in spite of all her troubles:

> The Church has lighted my way. Instead of struggling through a wilderness I have had a road—a road to virtue and truth. Only a road—the road to an end, not the end itself—the road to truth, not the fullness of truth itself.
>
> Without the Church should I have learned to serve, to pray, to love, to adore?
>
> If she offered expressions of truth, methods of service of which I could not avail myself, what matter, if she offered also the main direction of life?
>
> She taught me why I was in this world and what I had to do while I was in it; she taught me the right use of the body, without despising it, and its subjugation to soul; she taught me spiritual ambition, in virtue of my high destiny; she taught me to remember my own weakness and my inability to fulfill that destiny unaided; she taught me that God was my portion, and she offered me priceless help in the attainment of that portion; she told me what sin was, and she expected me to fall into it, but she offered me daily and hourly means of recovery from it; she spread out her sacramental system, with its visible and corporeal means of spiritual regeneration and strength and growth; . . . she taught me what Christ was and ever had been to mankind, and she kept His living remembrance in the Sacrament of the Eucharist; she told me of those who had almost transcended the bodily senses and heard words not given to man to utter. . . . In one word, she has taught me how to seek God. I believe that God's ways are not our ways and God's thoughts are not ours; that He can and does reveal Himself in countless ways. But to me He gave that way and showed no better one. . . . [39]

The concluding years of Maude Petre's life happened to coincide with immensely dramatic times in the history of England. The Petre diary reflects the turmoil, the terror, and resolve of the years from Munich to the Blitz.

After the Munich crisis, she wrote: "No use going into details—the crisis ended . . . the snubs to Chamberlain, the nagging and criticism . . . it disgusts one. Can they not see that a great step has been taken?"[40] Maybe alarmed by the general tenor of British attitudes, she noted in the diary on January 13, 1939, that she was at work on an article called "Is England Coming Down?" On August 23, 1939, one week before Hitler's invasion of Poland, Maude wrote "Hopes of peace grow less—but all is not lost." And then came the entry of September 3, 1939: "Sunday—war has been declared—after all our hopes. May it be short and may Germany be saved along with the rest of us."

Throughout 1940, the news grew increasingly dismal. The diary of May 22, 1940 reads: "Very terrible war news—the Germans are over-running France." And on June 9: "These are terrible times—our B.E.F. got away from Flanders almost entire—but total loss of equipment." The same day's entry notes her first learning of Loisy's death, which had occurred on the first of June. On July 17, 1940, Maude Petre wrote ominously:

> The general news has been so overwhelmingly bad that I lost all heart to write . . . the defeat and collapse and treachery of France have been a personal as well as a public sorrow. Her light has been put out. . . . I feel as though my heart would break.

MDP stayed in London at her home at 15 Campden Grove during the Blitz and her diary recorded the intensity of those early war years. Mrs. Cally Merewether, who knew her in those years, remembers that Maude Petre used to relate her conviction that it was just such a person as herself, without children or dependents, who should stay in London and risk death to perform the needed services. And so, although she was now nearly eighty, Maude Petre took on the volunteer work of fire-watcher, going around her neighborhood at nights complete with helmet and uniform trousers, carrying sand buckets.[41]

The Petre diary gives a chilling account of the horror of the Blitz. On August 30, 1940: "At night a bombing till 4 A.M.," and

on September 19, "the inferno goes on and the nights are hor-
rible." How did the aged Miss Petre keep her wits about her in
those days? She read St. Augustine to settle her nerves, a good
friend in London recalled.[42]

But all was not war work. In June, 1941, she had attended
and spoken at the World Congress of Religion at Oxford.[43] In October 1942 she spoke on von Hügel to the Friends' Centre and
later in the month visited in Scotland.[44] On December 11, 1942,
the diary recorded, Maude Petre had attended the World Congress of Faiths, and "had terrible breathlessness on way home in
the dark."[45]

In mid-December, Maude Petre was also busy preparing a
Christmas party for children at the London County Council nur-
sery where she attended as part of her war-work. At the nur-
sery, one of her contemporaries wrote, she "was idolized by the
children."[46]

On December 15, 1942, Maude wrote in her diary that she
had friends to lunch and tea. She then added:

> Have felt *very* poorly of late and unable to work. Have determined
> to pray for a few days and wait till I get God's touch and can work
> again.

It was to be the last entry. On December 16 she was seized by
another attack of breathlessness that took her life. She did not go
gently into that good night. James A. Walker, whom she had ap-
pointed her literary executor, observed that she died "struggling
for breath and waving her arms to the dawn that she did not live
to see."[47]

A brief announcement of Maude Petre's death appeared on
the front page of the London *Times* on December 17, 1942,
followed by a fuller obituary two days later. In Maude Petre, the
obituary noted, Modernism "found its most energetic English
apologist." Her letters to the *Times* during the Modernist crisis
"form an essential constituent of the literature of the movement,"
the obituary noted.[48]

Because Maude Petre died in the Westminster Diocese,
north of the Thames, it was possible for her to be accorded a Requiem Mass at Assumption Convent, Kensington Square. She was
buried in the Anglican Churchyard at Storrington, one grave

removed from Father Tyrrell.[49] Buried between them is their
mutual friend Arthur Bell. No priest was officially present at the
graveside service, because Bishop Amigo of Southwark (Storrington was under his jurisdiction) said he would allow Catholic
burial only if Miss Petre would be buried elsewhere than in prox-
imity to George Tyrrell.[50] Eventually a simple cross would be
erected over Maude Dominica Petre's grave, about two feet high,
and bearing only the initials "M.D.P." together with the traditional "R.I.P." and dates of birth and death.[51]

And so Maude Petre had followed her path of faith within
Catholic Christianity "however imperfectly," as she had once expressed the hope, "until my limbs carry me no further and the
path for me is ended."[52] At the end, in the procession to the grave,
the *De Profundis* and *Miserere* psalms were recited. And while
the body of Maude Petre was lowered into the ground, her two
nephews recited the Nicene Creed as she had directed.[53] A. L.
Lilley wrote of the funeral: "It was a beautiful farewell to one of
the rarest and most finely tempered Christian souls that our
generation has known."[54]

10

Conclusion:

MAUDE PETRE'S WAY OF FAITH

"A SOLITARY MAROONED PASSENGER, the sole living representative of what has come to be regarded as the lost cause of Modernism in the Catholic Church"[1] —that is how Maude Petre had described herself in her later years. Clearly enough, she persisted in considering herself faithful both to Modernism and Catholicism.

This strange religious ambivalence had run throughout Maude Petre's life: She came from a Cisalpine family tradition with all the attendant stress on the *limits* of the power of the Church, yet she grew up in a British Catholicism imbued with the spirit of men such as Cardinal Manning; she was tortured by religious doubt throughout her life, but held persistently to her way of faith, asking that the Nicene Creed be recited at her burial; she was *persona non grata* at the Eucharist south of the Thames, but at Kensington in the Westminster Diocese she received daily Communion and was described by a Carmelite priest as "a most holy and spiritual woman"; her funeral took place with a Catholic Requiem in one diocese, but without a priest in attendance at her graveside in another.

It is not without irony that this aristocratic British lady of such diversity had found multiplicity one of the great puzzles of life and that she saw humanity's drive for unity as fundamental to her religious nature. To seek for unity and precision in Maude Petre's own life and thought is not the lightest of tasks, yet, fundamental questions arise that must be confronted in concluding a study such as this one: To what extent did Maude Petre express Modernist convictions in her writings? What was her own share in the movement, and what originality of interpretation did she bring to Modernism? As one who maintained the Modernist spirit well over a generation after the end of the historical movement, what new emphasis or focus did she see in a world considerably changed from that which her early Modernist friends had known?

This study has not sought to prove either for or against the religious orthodoxy of Maude Petre, nor has it asked the question raised by some of her reviewers—whether she may rightly be called a Roman Catholic. Nor have these pages tried to establish how much of that for which the Modernists fought may have become acceptable in the Catholic Church after the Second Vatican Council, or how much must remain forever in opposition to the demands of Christian faith. The quest of this research has been a more modest one: it has sought to establish what was the role of Maude Petre in the Modernist movement.

MDP undoubtedly thought of herself as a proponent of Modernist aims. And her writings reveal her allegiance—at least in some measure—to certain elements of Modernism described by John Heaney, which were noted in chapter 3. Heaney, for instance, had spoken of Modernism in terms of the denial of the supernatural as an object of certain knowledge, of an immanence that reduced the Church to a mere civilizing phenomenon, and of the total emancipation of scientific research from dogma. By her separation of faith from certainty, Maude Petre did tend toward the denial of the supernatural as an object of certain knowledge, especially in terms of attempted proofs from external evidence. She did talk in terms of the Divine immanence, though not without a counterbalancing acknowledgment of transcendence; and she certainly conceived of the Church as more than a mere civilizing force in society, as will shortly be noted. On the third point, that of the emancipation of scientific research from dogma, Maude Petre held for the autonomous rights of history and science within their own realms. Unless Christianity was to be a phantom, she thought, it must be built upon certain bedrock historical facts; and a religion that depends on history, she had said, should also be subject to its laws. And yet she was convinced that the Modernists by their work were putting the truths of faith beyond the reach of criticism.

On several other points she enunciated over the years Petre would also find herself in conflict with *Pascendi, Lamentabili,* and their supporters. Thus, she deemed the Catholic Church vital but relative in its importance; similarly, she had written that she considered religious experience to be primary, and its dogmatic formulation relative. The Church's "mandate" was not to be found so much in external evidence as in its response to inner spiritual needs. One's allegiance should be stronger to the invisible Church than to the visible, and even within the visible Church, there must be an ultimacy to personal judgment.

There is salvation as well as revelation outside the Catholic communion, MDP had insisted, and allegiance to the Church is largely a matter of human choice. And hell, that frequent subject of Church preaching, cannot be eternal in its duration, she thought. If all these personal convictions of Maude Petre were not enough to fire the anger of her critics, there was always also her broadcasting of George Tyrrell's thought after his death, primarily through the publication of his *Christianity at the Cross-Roads* and the *Autobiography and Life of George Tyrrell*. Finally, there was her persistent refusal, throughout her life, to subscribe to the anti-Modernist oath and her local bishop's disciplinary action of refusing her the Eucharist in her home diocese of Southwark.

MDP had described her own share in the Modernist movement primarily through her friendship with von Hügel, Bremond, and Tyrrell. And in her writings and lectures she kept these men and their ideas before the public attention long after their strength and influence had gone into a kind of eclipse.

In the three decades between the imposition of the anti-Modernist oath in 1910 and Maude Petre's death in 1942, her voice would seem to have been one of the few in Britain to continue to champion the position of Modernism from a Catholic perspective. And during these years she came to feel, as she once expressed it, that some of the old disputes within the Church had become somewhat unimportant. In short, in her life and thought in those later years, Modernism took on the wider implication of reconciling not just Catholicism with modern thought and experience, but also of plumbing the depth of the relationship between human development and spiritual directedness. People stood in need, she said, of a developed and deepened sense of life; no subject that regards humanity was without religious significance. Accordingly, her own thought came to combine the political and social with the religious, for Maude Petre had insisted that if people were ever to attain a genuine human solidarity, they could do so only if they were grounded in the Divine. And it was to the Church that they looked if they sought to dwell on the ground of God's interplay with the human.

And so, Maude Petre's development in the conception of Modernism amounted to something more than just an anticipation of the secular-city mentality. She would find a direct correlation between what the Modernist had sought for the Church and what the idealist had sought in the First World War: a making of the world safe for freedom, for democracy. There had been the drive to bring the "mechanism of religious life into accordance with the free spontaneous life of heart and head in the believer." In a word, in Maude Petre's developed thought, Modernism became somewhat less parochial; it became more concerned with the discovery and enhancement of spiritual values in all people, both individually and in society. The Modernist drive to purify the Church, to free it from obsolete forms and positions, became more fully directed toward that end. The seed had been present in the earlier Modernists, with their solicitude to bring about new liberty and diversity within the Church, but in the work of Maude Petre, precisely because it was hammered out in the crucible of the chaos of later twentieth-century life, this solicitude focused more manifestly on the growth and spiritual development of all — not just those within the Catholic Church. A similar process was taking place in Loisy, who also lived until the time of the Second World War, but there was a critical difference. Maude Petre herself pointed out that Loisy had lost his hope that the Church could be the crucial, even the determining factor, in the transformation of humanity. MDP herself never lost that hope in the Church, and at one point she had defined Modernists precisely in terms of those who never wavered from such a deep-rooted hope.

All this points to the special centerpiece of Maude Petre's social, political, and spiritual thought: she made the Church the focus of all, as both her Modernist credo of 1918 and her Catholic apologia of 1937 suggest. We need, she had said, a shelter in the midst of immensity, some force that will lead humanity "to serve, to pray, to love and to adore," and it was in the Church that she had found such a force. Maude Petre had written a fine summary of her position in her 1923 Letter to Lord Halifax:

> The Church is our home—our ark on the immeasured waters. We know that we know but little, but we trust that the spiritual goods set before us are a pledge of those that are to be.

So, as she had done from the turn of the century onward, Maude Petre looked to the future possibilities of the Church as part of its very definition and she spoke of the importance of the invisible Church. Yet she did not conceive that the Church that would be operative in incarnational Christian reality in the world would be an abstraction. It would be essential, she said in her "Open Letter to Halifax," that the Church have a body; the "external differences" between the Christian Churches she would not permit to be disregarded or underemphasized. Within Roman Catholicism, Petre pointed to a very special strength: its dogged holding to the true Presence of Christ, both in the Eucharist and the Divinity doctrine.

As for hoped-for reforms, MDP had admitted that churches need time to adjust to change, and especially a Church as vast as the Roman Catholic needs time for the new to be assimilated through its many members. By 1937 when she wrote her autobiography, Petre already thought there were signs that people in the Church were thinking and speaking with more freedom because the Modernists had originally spoken out.

But the Church would have to be transformed in its own right if it were to serve humanity in the fullest sense. As Maude Petre so often wrote, the Church will have to suffer and die to attain new life. More especially, for Maude Petre, the Church would have to die to imposing itself beyond its own domain. If Christology had been the most troublesome question of Modernism for Maude Petre—especially insofar as the scientific challenges cut into the realm of devotion and piety—it was because it was but the direct exemplification of a deeper problem of the rights of historical research and their relationship to the rights of belief. When the logic was pushed still farther back, then, Maude Petre admitted that the root problem of Modernism had been the limits of authority within the Church. The Church, she thought, had its own proper domain; it was rightly supreme, she had written, with regard to eternal truths which it was bound to protect. But let the Church step over into total assurance in other domains, let it try to dictate to science from the groundwork of its theology, and soon that same Church finds itself confronted with what Maude Petre had called unconscious Modernism, the crying (though often unspoken) need of the common people whose devotional life and moral perspectives are upset by the inflexibility of the Church. In spite of it all, though, Petre found hope for the Church that she said was glorious because of the seed it bears, though lowly because of the imperfection of its own response.

This discussion of the Church in Maude Petre's understanding brings into perspective yet another facet of her Modernist interpretation. Following in the tradition of Tyrrell, she saw the rights of devotion and the spiritual life as especially paramount. Her whole discussion of "unconscious Modernism" in her 1937 work was meant to point out that in both Loisy and Tyrrell there was a response not to some esoteric need of a few intellectuals in the Modernist crisis; rather, she suggested, they sought to preserve a devotional basis for all Christians. She herself had written that one ultimately had to choose between the fabrications of some critics and the Christ whom the Church had unceasingly put forth for worship. And she had written in her autobiography that piety preserved more faith than orthodoxy. Here, then, is yet another evidence that Maude Petre's vision for the Church was that it be something more profound than simply a civilizing force. It fostered the devotional life, provided the healthy tension needed to prevent religious life from trailing away into some nebulous state, and offered the possibility of a matrix out of which a new religious consciousness would emerge.

As her own particular type of Modernism developed, then, MDP envisioned the possible coming of a new religion, and she could not preclude the possibility of new revelation. What structure such a religion might have was as yet unknown, and, as she once suggested, a pope may not have a place in such a coming religion. At other times, she spoke of the papacy as the one possible point around which humanity could rally in its drive to shatter its collective selfishness. Whatever form the religion might take, though, Maude Petre looked toward Christianity as its greatest element. And shortly before her death she had studied the

Beatitudes of Jesus as the only possible workable basis on which
might be founded a truly human society.

Maude Petre may have been an idealist; she may have been
unorthodox. Probably neither designation would have deeply
disturbed her. The adjective she would probably have best liked
applied herself would have been *independent*, a word that was frequent in her vocabulary throughout her life; it was part of her in-
heritance, no doubt, as a hearty daughter of the Cisalpine, old
English Catholic tradition. Especially after the condemnation of
Modernism, Petre found herself in a position of independence—
standing out as that solitary marooned passenger.

After the fallout in the wake of the Modernist controversy,
after Tyrrell's death and after Loisy's departure, after so many
others either left the Church or became silent, Maude Petre persisted in her independent course:

> Some Modernists gave up faith for history; some gave up history
> for faith. Some sought a method of evasion in a philosophy of
> pure symbolism. Some kept both faith and problem.[2]

It was to this last group that Maude Petre herself belonged; she
kept both faith and problem in the conviction that in her faith lay
buried the answers to as yet unanswered questions. As she stressed
more than once, the Modernist could never hold that the axe had
been laid to the root of belief because the roots ran too deep to
be struck such a decisive blow. This, then, was Maude Petre's independent course—not to yield all to a Church that she thought
was overreaching itself; not to yield all to science that was both
inconclusive and but one form of human knowing.

The role of Maude Petre in the Modernist movement, then,
cannot be found in any forceful direct influence she might have
had on a wide theological audience. The facts that all her books
went out of print and that no previous critical survey has been
done of her work only indicate strongly that Maude Petre cannot
be said to have left many disciples. But, surely it is clear by now
that her role is to be sought in another direction than that of wide
acclaim—either critical or popular.

Maude Petre saw her own role during the Modernist crisis
itself in her relationship with her friends von Hügel, Bremond,
and Tyrrell. She shared many of their ideas and wrote on them,

of course. Yet her main book during the crisis, *Catholicism and Independence* did not so much take up the specific issues of immanence, or exegesis; rather it was a hearty defense of those who did raise such issues in the Church. During the crisis itself, then, she may be said to have played a supportive role, encouraging Tyrrell especially to hold to his Catholic faith, fighting after Tyrrell's death for the vindication of his beliefs in her attempt to get him a Catholic burial. If Tyrrell had received a Catholic burial, she thought it would have established a principle that ultramontanism was not the only form of Catholicism, for it was against ultramontanism that she considered Tyrrell locked in combat.

If during the crisis itself Petre had played a supportive role in the Modernist offensive, in the second phase, the "fallout" or aftermath period, she was both propagator and symbol. In her research on Tyrrell and in her publications of his work she propagated his thought and sought to insure the continuance of his battle against the forces of "Vaticanism." And in her refusal to take the oath against Modernism after her bishop failed to assure her of its *de fide* character, she became, as already noted, an international symbol of resistance to the imposition of an oath which, she thought, made all Catholics suspect save the pope himself.

And finally, in the period between the wars, Maude Petre played out the last part of her role in the Modernist movement—that of critic or transformer. For in turning her attention to the plight of humanity after the wars and to the struggles of people to achieve more fully human societies, she saw a new imperative for the Church. She could now allow that there had been excesses in Modernism, but the main actors in the drama had helped the Church to see its own widened role. By rooting men and women in the ground of transcendence, the Church must help them to become more fully human. What had earlier been a battle that was seen more narrowly in terms of how to transform the Church for the growth of its own members now took on wider dimensions: The Church must become the vehicle to carry humanity to deeper personal integrity, to fuller social solidarity, and ultimately to a personal relationship with God.

Supporter, Propagator, Symbol, Critic, and Transformer—Maude Petre filled all these roles at some time within the Modernist movement. And she carried out each role with a full conviction that her labor was directed toward a new fullness of life and nobility of mission for the Catholic Church. Throughout all the ambivalence of her eighty years, she held steadfastly to the Church that had nurtured her, and throughout her adult life, she held steadfastly to the vision of the future which Modernism inspired in her. She followed this course, as she said, until her limbs would carry her no more and the path for her was ended.

Even now, some forty years after that path ended for Maude Petre, perhaps no better conclusion could be found to summarize her unshakable fidelity both to Catholicism and to Modernism than the words that she herself wrote in concluding an article about Tyrrell and von Hügel in 1927:

> Never has human life changed more rapidly than during the last years, and new light may yet be shed upon our whole destiny. But nothing can alter the radical aspiration of the human heart, and it was for these that the Modernist contended, and for the sake of which he endured the cramping torture of ecclesiastical institutions, because in spite of their limitations, he found in them a support in the passage through this dark and troubled life; he found through them, the grace to live, the courage to die.[3]

Notes

Introduction

1. As early as his 1934 study, *The Modernist Movement in the Roman Church* (Cambridge: University Press, 1934), p. 202, Alec Vidler spoke of Maude Petre as one of the more "conspicuous" members of the movement in England. Later, in *A Variety of Catholic Modernists* (Cambridge: University Press, 1970), p. 109, Vidler spoke of her as one of the "major" English Modernists. In the massive study of Emile Poulat, *Histoire, dogme et critique dans la Crise Moderniste* (Paris: Casterman, 1962), p. 18, one finds MDP listed near the top echelon of British Modernism; still, she is not studied in her own right.

2. At least two articles have appeared since Maude Petre's death: James A. Walker, "Maude Petre: A Memorial Tribute," *Hibbert Journal* 41 (April 1943), 340–46. Walker was named MDP's literary executor in her will of 1939. See also Robert Hamilton, "Faith and Knowledge: The Autobiography of Maude Petre," *Downside Review* 85 (April 1967), 148–59. In addition, Petre is mentioned in a lengthy article on Henri Bremond that appeared in 1954. See H. C. Snape, "Portrait of a Devout Humanist," *Harvard Theological Review* 47 (January 1954), 15–53. My own article "Maude Petre's Modernism" appeared in *America*, May 16, 1981, pp. 403–6.

Most of the references to be found in the standard writers on Modernism (Houtin, Lilley, Reardon, Rivière) are only to Petre's role as biographer and friend of George Tyrrell. Throughout the three volumes of Loisy's *Mémoires*, however (Paris: Nourry, 1931), references to Maude Petre are frequent as well as fond.

3. Walker, "Maude Petre: A Memorial Tribute," p. 344.

4. Regrettably, only few women have been recognized as significant contributors to the theological enterprise in this period. Among

those names that would come immediately to mind are Edith Stein (1891–1942), Evelyn Underhill (1875–1941) and Simone Weil (1909–1943).

5. For further examples of the strongly independent strain of lay Catholics in England see E. I. Watkin, *Roman Catholicism in England: From the Reformation to 1950* (London: Oxford University Press, 1957).

6. The literature on the history of English Catholicism from the Reformation, through Emancipation, to the restoration of the hierarchy is quite large. Some of the representative titles include: Charles Butler, *Historical Memoirs Respecting the English, Irish and Scottish Catholics from the Reformation to the Present Time* (London: John Murray, 1819); Philip Caraman, *The Other Face: Catholic Life under Elizabeth I* (London: Longmans, 1960), and by the same author *Years of Siege: Catholic Life from James I to Cromwell* (London: Longmans, 1966); Owen Chadwick, *The Victorian Church*, 2 vols. (New York: Oxford University Press, 1966); Denis Gwynn, *The Struggle for Catholic Emancipation (1750–1829)* (London: Longmans, Green, 1928); also by Gwynn, *A Hundred Years of Catholic Emancipation* (London: Longmans, Green, 1929). A recent, carefully detailed study of these centuries is John Bossy's, *The English Catholic Community 1570–1850* (New York: Oxford University Press, 1976).

7. Watkin, *Roman Catholicism in England*, p. 88.

8. Ibid., p. 131.

9. James J. Hennesey, S.J., has written, "the spirit which developed in the early American church was one that looked for a measure of internal autonomy." "National Traditions and the First Vatican Council," *Archivium Historicae Pontificiae* 7 (1969), 508.

10. Maude Petre, *The Ninth Lord Petre* (London: SPCK, 1928), p. 174.

11. Ibid., p. 324.

12. Ibid., p. 219.

13. Ibid., pp. 126–27.

14. Holmes, *More Roman than Rome* (London: Burns and Oates, 1978). See also M. Nédoncelle, ed., *L'Ecclésiologie au XIXᵉ Siècle*, Unam Sanctam, No. 34 (Paris: Editions du Cerf, 1960).

15. For life and critiques of Manning, see Shane Leslie, *Henry Edward Manning: His Life and Labours* (New York: Kenedy, 1954); V. McClelland, *Cardinal Manning: His Public Life and Influence* (London: Oxford University Press, 1962); and Edmund Purcell, *Life of Cardinal Manning*, 2 vols. (New York: Macmillan, 1898).

With reference to the general tenor of English Catholic life and thought in the mid- and late nineteenth century, see Josef Altholz, *The Liberal Catholic Movement and Its Contributors* (London: Burns and Oates, 1962). This provides a picture of attempts by such men as Acton, Newman, and Simpson to publish "liberal journals." A general account of the First Vatican Council, though with particular attention given to British participation, is to be found in Cuthbert Butler, *The Vatican Council*, 2 vols. (London: Longmans, Green, 1930).

16. Owen Chadwick, *The Victorian Church*, I, 281–84.

17. Some sense of Cardinal Manning's perspective is to be found by a careful reading of three of his pastoral letters published at the time of the Council: Henry Edward Manning, *Petri Privilegium* (London: Longmans, Green, 1871).

18. Purcell, *Life of Cardinal Manning*, II, 458–59.

19. For material on Acton's thought on the Church and authority, see his *Essays on Church and State* (New York: Crowell, 1968).

20. In addition to the material in Manning's three pastorals cited above in note 17, there are other writings by the cardinal that make significant comment on the Council: *The True Story of the Vatican Council* (London: Henry S. King, 1877) and *The Vatican Decrees in Their Bearing on Civil Allegiance* (New York: Catholic Publication Society, 1875).

21. Maude Petre, *My Way of Faith* (London: J. M. Dent and Sons, 1937), p. 18. For the rest of this study this work will be noted simply as *My Way of Faith*.

22. Petre, *The Ninth Lord Petre*, p. xiii.

1. Victorian Sunset

1. *My Way of Faith*, p. 13. See also *The Ninth Lord Petre*, pp. 14–29.

2. *My Way of Faith*, p. 29.

3. MDP wrote of her father: "He was just, charitable and true; but his feet were soberly planted on the earth, and my silly head was in the clouds so I did not appreciate him." Ibid., p. 28.

4. Ibid., p. 61.

5. Ibid., pp. 65–66.

6. Ibid., p. 96.

7. Ibid., pp. 129, 123.

8. Ibid., p. 129.

9. Ibid., p. 162.

10. Ibid.

11. Ibid., p. 163.

12. Ibid.

13. Petre identifies the priest only as "Father Humphrey." His profile fits precisely, however, that offered by David Schultenover of Father William Humphrey. See Schultenover's very careful study *George Tyrrell: In Search of Catholicism* (Shepherdstown, W. Va.: Patmos Press, 1981), pp. 101, 164, 393.

14. Ibid., p. 393.

15. *My Way of Faith*, p. 168. The doctrinal statement is to be found in *The Church Teaches*, trans. John F. Clarkson, S.J., et al. (St. Louis: Herder Book Co., 1954), p. 28.

16. *My Way of Faith*, p. 172.

17. Ibid., p. 168.

18. See James Walker's introductory chapter, "Maude Petre," in MDP's posthumous text *Alfred Loisy: His Religious Significance* (Cambridge: University Press, 1944), p. ix.

19. *My Way of Faith*, p. 173.

20. Ellen Leonard, *George Tyrrell and the Catholic Tradition* (New York: Paulist Press, 1982), pp. 11 ff. See also Schultenover's second chapter "The Orthodox Years," pp. 28–47.

21. "Victor Hugo," *Month* 54 (July 1885), 319, 322.

22. "Carlyle on Religious Ceremonies," *Month* 55 (November 1885), 318.

23. The source for the dates of MDP's life in the Society were provided in letters written me by Agnes Keenan, Assistant General of the Society in Paris (dated March 18, 1971), and by S. M. Watson, English Provincial in London (dated April 7, 1971). The latter observed that Maude Petre never took perpetual vows, nor asked to take them.

24. A brief explanation of the Society is to be found in "Society of the Daughters of the Heart of Mary: A Short Sketch," a pamphlet published in 1963. The sketch notes that those who are "too independent" are not well suited to the religious life. Agnes Keenan, in the letter cited in the note above, indicated that Petre was refused permission to renew her vows because of her publication, without permission, of *Catholicism and Independence* in 1907.

25. James Walker, "Maude Petre: A Memorial Tribute," p. 345. Agnes Keenan, however, wrote that the archives of the Society contained "little information about her activities." And S. M. Watson said

in her letter: "I can find no record of her having taken any active part in any of the works of the Society. I understand that she had certain gifts of intellect which were unfortunately diverted away after she came under the influence of Fr. Tyrrell."

26. British Museum, Add. MS. 45,476, Vaughan-Petre, March 20, 1898.

27. "Shades of the Prison House," *Month* 93 (April 1899), 389.

28. British Museum, Add. MS. 52,367, Petre Papers, Vol. 1 contains letters from Tyrrell to Petre from 1898 to 1908.

29. British Museum, Add. MS. 52,380, Petre Papers, Vol. 14, contains letters from Bremond to Petre from 1900 to 1935.

30. British Museum, Add. MSS. 45,361–62 contain letters from von Hügel to Petre from 1899 to 1922.

31. *My Way of Faith*, p. 90.

32. December 16, 1899, pp. 797–800. This was also printed in George Tyrrell, *Essays on Faith and Immortality*, arranged by Maude Petre (London: E. Arnold, 1914), pp. 158–71.

33. British Museum, Add. MS. 52,367, Petre Papers, Vol. 1, Tyrrell-Petre, August 15, 1900.

34. In the British Museum, the diaries constitute Add. MSS. 52,372–79 and cover the period from 1900 to Maude Petre's death in 1942. There are eight volumes with a total of well over a thousand handwritten pages.

2. New Century—New Influences

1. British Museum, Add. MS. 52,372, Petre Papers, Vol. 6, Diary 1, July 23, 1901. MDP takes note of the first anniversary of the retreat.

2. *My Way of Faith*, pp. 270, 272.

3. Ibid., p. 272.

4. Ibid., pp. 276–77.

5. Ibid., p. 277.

6. Letter to the Editor, *Tablet* 116 (November 12, 1910), 780. This article appears in Cambridge University Library, George Tyrrell Press Cuttings, Book 3.

7. *My Way of Faith*, p. 281.

8. British Museum, Add. MS. 52,372, Petre Papers, Vol. 6, Diary 1, September 27, 1900.

9. *My Way of Faith*, pp. 274–75.

10. British Museum, Add. MS. 52,367, Petre Papers, Vol. 1, Tyrrell-Petre, December 18, 1900.

11. *My Way of Faith*, pp. 129–30.

12. Ibid., p. 276. "And from that time forth my friendship with George Tyrrell took on ever increasingly the character of a spiritual vocation" (p. 276). For material on the celibacy vow, British Museum, Add. MS. 52,372, Petre Papers, Vol. 6, May 23, 1901. In January 1902, MDP published a defense of celibacy in "Human Love and Divine Love," *Catholic World* 74 (January 1902), 442–53.

13. *My Way of Faith*, p. 279. Also, see British Museum, Add. MS. 52,372, Petre Papers, Vol. 6, Diary 1, November 1, 1900. But there was not only fear; there was occasional comfort: "G.T. gave me great comfort by one word—that for him it is Catholicism or nothing." British Musuem, Add. MS. 52,374, Petre Papers, Vol. 7, Diary 3, March 16, 1908.

14. *My Way of Faith*, p. 273.

15. Ibid., p. 271. "Tyrrell and I were as unalike as possible in temperament and character; he was elusive, I was direct; he was rebellious, I was law-abiding; he was subtle, I was simple; he was utterly without self-regard, I was self-conscious."

16. Ibid., p. 283.

17. British Museum, Add. MS. 44,929, Tyrrell-von Hügel, June 9, 1906.

18. British Museum, Add. MS. 52,374, Petre Papers, Vol. 7, June 17, 1906.

19. Von Hügel's works were extensive. For a bibliography, see John J. Heaney, *The Modernist Crisis: von Hügel* (Washington: Corpus Books, 1968).

20. *My Way of Faith*, p. 254.

21. Ibid., p. 254.

22. Ibid., pp. 256–57.

23. Ibid., p. 258.

24. Maude Petre wrote to Canon Lilley: "Père Bremond is not a Modernist, nor seriously interested in Modernist questions." (Ibid., p. 269). Bremond's most important output was his massive study of seventeenth-century French literature of spirituality: *L'Histoire litteraire du sentiment religieux en France*, 11 vols. (Paris: Bloud et Gay, 1916–1932).

25. *My Way of Faith*, p. 264.

26. Ibid., p. 265.

27. Ibid., p. 253.

28. The quotation from MDP comes from a discussion of her study of the "Love Letters" and of other novels popular in the Modernist period. See Anne Louis-David, "The Latest from Mudies," *Month*, 2nd n.s. 1 (May 1970), 294.

29. Maude Petre, "An Englishwoman's Love Letters," *Month* 97 (February 1901), 120.

30. Ibid., p. 121.

31. Ibid., p. 124.

32. Ibid.

33. British Museum, Add. MS. 52,367, Petre Papers, Vol. 1, Tyrrell-Petre, August 24, 1900.

34. Bernard Reardon, *Roman Catholic Modernism* (London: Adam and Charles Black, 1970), p. 54. For a more readily approachable sample of Blondel's thought than the notoriously difficult *L'Action* one might consult his *Letter on Apologetics and History and Dogma*, ed. and trans. Alexander Dru and Illtyd Trethowan (New York: Holt, Rinehart and Winston, 1964). On Blondel, see Henri Bouillard, *Blondel and Christianity* (Washington: Corpus, 1969) and James Somerville, *Total Commitment* (Washington: Corpus, 1968).

35. The charge of total immanence was made in both anti-Modernist papal documents of 1907. For English texts of both *Pascendi Dominici Gregis* and *Lamentabili Sane*, see the pamphlet *Pascendi* (Washington: N.C.W.C., 1963). All references in this study will be to this N.C.W.C. text.

36. *Weekly Register*, November 22, 1901, pp. 635–36; November 29, 1901, pp. 669–70; December 6, 1901, pp. 701–2.

37. *Weekly Register*, November 22, 1901, p. 636.

38. Ibid., December 6, 1901, p. 701.

39. British Museum, Add. MS. 52,372, Petre Papers, Vol. 6, Diary 1, February 18, 1901.

40. MDP comments on this book of Loisy's: "Loisy leaves us all we really want in the Bible" (ibid., December 11, 1901).

41. British Museum, Add. MS. 52,373, Petre Papers, Vol. 7, Diary 2, February 16, 1903. Maude Petre found the Buddha on the whole disappointing. Nirvana, she thought, revealed a hidden desire for immortality, because the Buddhist objects, not to life, but to its transitoriness. The references for the list of readings are to be found *passim* throughout the diaries.

42. "Human Love and Divine Love," p. 442.

43. *Monthly Register*, 1902, p. 265.

44. Ibid., p. 266.

45. Ibid.

46. Ibid., p. 267.

47. "Unum Necessarium," *Monthly Register*, 1902, p. 226.

48. "Alma Mater," *Weekly Register*, March 14, 1902, p. 317.

3. Emerging Conflicts, 1903–1907

1. Even though Modernism and Protestant liberalism responded to similar problems, it would be a mistake to identify too readily the two movements. Of course both tried to deal with certain common problems: Scripture criticism and the relationship of faith and history. But it is important to note that Loisy's *L'Evangile et L'Eglise*, which was so prominent in the Modernist controversy, was written against one of Harnack's central positions: that there is an essence of Christianity detached from its development in history; thus the problem of historical criticism is obliterated by making history nonessential. But truth is only to be found in Catholic fullness through history and tradition, Loisy wrote: "we know Christ only by the tradition, across the tradition, and in the tradition of the primitive Christians." Alfred Loisy, *The Gospel and the Church* (New York: Scribner's, 1904), p. 13.

2. Alfred Loisy, *Autour d'un petit livre* (Paris: Alphonse Picard, 1903). This second of the "little red books"—so called from the color of their binding—was never translated into English.

3. For a treatment of the dispute between Tyrrell and his Jesuit superiors over the *Letter*, see *Autobiography and Life of George Tyrrell* (New York: Longmans, Green, 1912), II, 249–55.

4. *A Much-Abused Letter* (London: Longmans, Green, 1906), p. 81.

5. Quoted in Henri Daniel-Rops, *A Fight for God* (London: J. M. Dent, 1966), p. 227.

6. Ibid. For the original text of *E Supremi Apostolatus Cathedra*, see *Acta Sanctae Sedis*, 1903–4, pp. 129–59. For an English translation, see Vincent Yzermans, *All Things in Christ* (Westminster, Md.: Newman Press, 1954), pp. 3–12.

7. See Daniel-Rops, *A Fight for God*, p. 227.

8. For insightful coverage of the ecclesial and theological situations antecedent to Modernism one could consult Gerald McCool's *Catholic Theology in the Nineteenth Century: The Quest for a Unitary Method* (New

York: Seabury, 1977) and Owen Chadwick's *The Secularization of the European Mind in the Nineteenth Century* (Cambridge: University Press, 1978).

Standard overviews of Modernism, some previously cited, include Jean Rivière's *Le Modernisme dans l'Eglise* (Paris: Letouzey et Ané, 1929); Alec Vidler's *The Modernist Movement in the Roman Church*; Emile Poulat's *Histoire, dogme et critique dans la Crise Moderniste*; and Bernard Reardon's anthology with thorough introduction, *Roman Catholic Modernism*.

More recent comprehensive studies of the movement include those of Roger Aubert, "The Modernist Crisis," in Herbert Jedin and John Dolan, eds., *The Church in the Industrial Age* (New York: Crossroad, 1981), pp. 420-80; and "The Modernist Crisis and the Integrist Reaction," in Aubert et al., *The Church in a Secularised Society* (New York: Paulist Press, 1978), pp. 186-203; Gabriel Daly, *Transcendence and Immanence: A Study in Catholic Modernism and Integralism* (Oxford: Clarendon Press, 1980); Thomas Loome, *Liberal Catholicism, Reform Catholicism, Catholic Modernism* (Mainz: Matthias-Grunewald, 1979).

Helpful encyclopedia summaries are to be found in John Heaney's article "Modernism" in volume 9 of the 1966 *New Catholic Encyclopedia* as well as in its 1974 revision in volume 16; and John Ratte's "Modernism in the Christian Church" in the 1973 *Dictionary of the History of Ideas*. For the context of literary modernism, an indispensable source is Malcolm Bradbury and James McFarlane, eds., *Modernism: 1890-1930* (New York: Penguin, 1976). For an idea of the rapid expansion of Modernist researches, see the bibliographies in Ronald Burke and George Gilmore, eds., *Current Research in Roman Catholic Modernism* (Spring Hill, Ala.: College Press, 1980).

9. This twenty year period is adopted by Reardon, *Roman Catholic Modernism*, p. 10.

It is one of the perennial difficulties of twentieth-century Catholic historical studies to produce a satisfactory definition or description of Modernism. One of the tasks of this study will be to introduce more readily into the proceedings Maude Petre's own definitions and historical perspectives on the movement (chapter 8).

10. Karl Rahner and Herbert Vorgrimler, "Modernism," *Theological Dictionary* (New York: Herder and Herder, 1965), p. 290.

11. Reardon, *Roman Catholic Modernism*, p. 9.

12. Heaney, *The Modernist Crisis: von Hügel*, p. 232.

13. Ibid.

14. Rahner and Vorgrimler, *Theological Dictionary*, p. 290.

15. MDP attributed the quote in her diary to a Dr. Hedley. British Museum, Add. MS. 52,373, Petre Papers, Vol. 7, Diary 2, October 20, 1904. Dr. Hedley was J. C. Hedley, Roman Catholic Bishop of Newport (England) from 1881 to 1915.

16. *Dublin Review* 135 (October 1904), 431.

17. Ibid., p. 432.

18. Ibid., p. 433.

19. *Catholic World* 79 (August 1904), 683.

20. *Where Saints Have Trod* (London: Catholic Truth Society, 1903), p. 1.

21. Ibid., p. 2.

22. Ibid.

23. Ibid., p. 4.

24. Ibid.

25. Ibid., pp. 10–11.

26. Ibid., p. 11.

27. Ibid. She also commented: "There is nothing actually ennobling in mere separation and seclusion from the life of humanity at large; that were a loss rather than a gain unless it substituted a deeper sympathy with the more fundamental interests of mankind" (p. 8).

28. Ibid., p. 12.

29. Ibid., p. 65.

30. Ibid., p. 66.

31. Ibid., p. 68.

32. Ibid., p. 70.

33. Ibid., p. 76.

34. Ibid.

35. Ibid., p. 92.

36. Ibid., pp. 87–88.

37. Ibid., pp. 105–6.

38. Ibid., p. 18.

39. Also in 1904, MDP published a 48-page pamphlet called "Devotional Essays" for the Catholic Truth Society of London which was derived from *Where Saints Have Trod*. In 1903 she had produced another pamphlet for the Catholic Truth Society called "The Temperament of Doubt," which became the basis for the chapter of the same name in *Catholicism and Independence* (1907) and will be considered there in its turn.

40. Maude Petre, *The Soul's Orbit* (London: Longmans, Green, 1904), pp. 4–5. Italics are mine.

41. See note 4 above.

42. British Museum, Add. MS. 52,373, Petre Papers, Vol. 7, Diary 2, February 7, 1904.

43. Ibid., September 2, 1904.

44. Ibid., October 20, 1904.

45. Ibid., November 16, 1904.

46. *The Soul's Orbit*, pp. 9, 11.

47. Ibid., pp. 11–12.

48. Ibid., p. 17.

49. "Americanism" had stressed the active virtues over the passive, and had held more for the value of self-directedness in determining the work of the Holy Spirit as opposed to the constant need for external direction. The life of Isaac Hecker (1819–1888), a convert to Catholicism and founder of the Paulists, had supposedly shown such Americanist tendencies, at least according to an appreciative biography written shortly after Hecker's death. See Walter Elliott, *The Life of Father Hecker* (New York: Columbus Press, 1891). A French edition brought on a strong Roman reaction. Pope Leo XIII sent *Testem Benevolentiae* to Cardinal Gibbons in 1899, pointing out the dangers of "Americanism." For a detailed discussion of the Americanist controversy, see Thomas McAvoy, *The Great Crisis in American Catholic History 1895–1900* (Chicago: Henry Regnery, 1957).

50. *The Soul's Orbit*, p. 141.

51. Ibid., p. 147.

52. Ibid., p. 183.

53. Ibid.

54. Ibid., pp. 183–84.

55. *The Gospel and the Church*, p. 166: "It is certain, for instance, that Jesus did not systematize beforehand the constitution of the Church as that of a government established on earth and destined to endure for a long series of centuries."

56. *The Soul's Orbit*, p. 180. And further, "It was only the gradual, but quite inevitable (and in many ways desirable) dying down of inspiration that allowed and necessitated the development of that supernatural institution, which was destined to be the organ of Christ's Spirit" (pp. 180–81).

57. *Pascendi*, N.C.W.C. Edition, p. 16.

58. Petre, *The Soul's Orbit*, p. 174.

59. Ibid., p. 184.

60. Ibid., p. 200.

61. *Dublin Review* 137 (October 1905), 401.

62. Petre, *The Soul's Orbit*, pp. 47–48.

63. *American Ecclesiastical Review* 32 (February 1905), 196–98.

64. British Museum, Add. MS. 52,373, Petre Papers, Vol. 7, Diary 2, February 2, 1905. She had noted a month earlier that she was resigning for reasons of conscience—being unfitted, she said, in mind and body. Ibid., January 18, 1905.

65. In her letter to me of March 18, 1971, Agnes Keenan noted Petre's maintenance of the councilor's office and mentioned that the resignation from the superiority was "for reasons of health."

66. Maude Petre, "De Profundis," *Month* 105 (April 1905), 387.

67. Maude Petre, "Pessimism in Its Relation to Asceticism," *Catholic World* 81 (April 1905), 43.

68. Maude Petre, "Studies on Friedrich Nietzsche: VI–Nietzsche the Anti-Christian," *Catholic World* 83 (June 1906), 347.

69. Ibid., pp. 354–55.

70. *Il Rinnovamento* 1 (May 1907), 572.

71. Ibid., pp. 573, 576.

72. British Museum Add. MS. 52,373, Vol. 7, Diary 2, March 15, 1905.

73. Ibid., April 16, 1905.

74. Ibid., April 14, 1906.

4. Catholicism and Independence

1. British Museum, Add. MS. 52,374 Petre Papers, Vol. 8, Diary 3, March 8, 1908 and June 17, 1908.

2. In her letter of March 18, 1971, Agnes Keenan explains: "There was no intervention from Rome. When a person enters religious life she contracts to live under obedience. Miss Petre published her book without the permission of her superiors and for that reason was refused her vows." MDP had written to Canon A. L. Lilley on December 24, 1907: "My book has already cost me the severance from a religious association to which I have belonged about 15 years, and which I ruled for 10 years." St. Andrew's University Library, Lilley Papers, Petre-

Lilley, December 24, 1907. For a brief description of Canon Lilley's place in the Modernist movement, see Vidler, *A Variety of Catholic Modernists*, pp. 126–33.

3. Maude Petre, *Catholicism and Independence* (London: Longmans, Green, 1907), pp. x–xi.

4. The substance of "The Temperament of Doubt" had appeared in a Catholic Truth Society pamphlet of the same name in 1903. Apparently an even earlier draft was in existence, for as early as 1901 Baron von Hügel had written a glowing appreciation to Maude Petre: "your Temperament of Doubt . . . there is not a word in it that belongs to the category of mere words; it is as organized and unified as life itself from which it comes and to which it leads." British Museum, Add. MS. 42,361, von Hügel-Petre, May 18, 1901.

Tyrrell had also commented on the work in an undated letter from the Jesuit's Farm Street Church, London: "I like this more than I can tell. It is very bold and yet—very sound . . . you must, I think, in order to evade the theological philistines make it clear that you are speaking of suggested [?] doubt and of accepted [?] doubt, else will come I know not what anathemas." Tyrrell's writing was not always completely legible. British Museum, Add. MS. 52,367, Petre Papers, Vol. 1 Tyrrell-Petre, n.d. Although the letter is undated, it was in the packet of letters between the dates May 28, 1900 and August 15, 1900.

5. *Catholicism and Independence*, p. 9.

6. Ibid., p. 21.

7. Ibid., p. 31.

8. Ibid.

9. *My Way of Faith*, p. 341.

10. John Lancaster Spalding, *Education and the Higher Life* (Chicago: A. C. McClure, 1890), p. 14.

11. *Catholicism and Independence*, p. 33.

12. Ibid., p. 39.

13. Ibid., p. 44.

14. Ibid., pp. 44–45.

15. Ibid., pp. 47–48, 52.

16. Ibid., p. 49.

17. Ibid.

18. Ibid.

19. Ibid., p. 64.

20. Ibid., p. 67.

21. Ibid., p. 69.

22. "In so far as we obey the spiritual Church we obey that which is best in ourselves; she represents to us that higher law which is in our own soul as in the souls of all who belong to her. . . . The spiritual Church can do no wrong; her rights over us are simply co-extensive with the rights of our conscience and with our own actual participation in life and being." Ibid., p. 67.

23. Ibid., p. 69.

24. Ibid., p. 101.

25. Ibid., p. 70.

26. Ibid., pp. 100–101.

27. Ibid., p. 101.

28. Ibid., pp. 103–4.

29. Ibid., pp. 104–5.

30. Ibid., p. 106.

31. Ibid.

32. Ibid., p. 153.

33. Ibid., pp. 152–53.

34. Ibid., p. 158.

35. Ibid., pp. 172–73. The language MDP employed is strikingly like that of some theologians in the mid-1960s in a "world come of age."

36. Ibid., pp. 173–74.

37. Ibid., p. 174.

38. Of the encyclical, Maude Petre wrote in her diary: "The Encyclical has appeared this last week—as extreme and impossible as was expected." British Museum, Add. MS. 52,374, Diary 3, September 22, 1907. In November she wrote, after announcement of another *Motu Proprio* from Rome: "but it all becomes more and more mad and one cannot but ask what will remain of the official Church at all?" Diary 3, November 24, 1907.

39. St. Andrew's University Library, Lilley Papers, Petre-Lilley, August 17, 1907. MDP observed in this same letter to Lilley that she thought the essential thing needed at the moment is "a simple protest for the rights of truth and criticism and liberty." She added, a few lines later: "After all, what we really agree on, is our view as to the excesses of authority and its invasion of a domain where the only authority is objective certainty and conviction."

40. Ibid., December 24, 1907.

41. Ibid.

5. The Death of Tyrrell

1. Bibliotheque Nationale, Paris, N.A.F. 15,600, Loisy Papers, Vol. 27, Petre-Loisy, June 21, 1908: "Je ne suis pas, et je ne serai jamais—une savante . . . mais j'ai l'amour de la verité." There are 210 pages of letters in the collection of Petre's letters to Loisy. The first is dated March 16, 1908, the last, June 15, 1940.

2. "Ossequio o idolatria?" *Nova et Vetera* 2 (October 1908), 205–10. Von Hügel found the article "admirable." British Museum, Add. MS. 45,361, von Hügel-Petre, November 12, 1908.

3. "Ossequio o idolatria?" pp. 207–8.

4. Ibid., p. 209. "O cuore del Santo Patre, riscalda il mio cuore—fammi amare quel che tu ami—fammi amare gli eretici e i modernisti nella maniera in cui tu li ami, *e non diversamente.*"

5. British Museum, Add. MS. 52,374, Petre Papers, Vol. 8, Diary 3, June 10, 14, 1906.

6. Ibid., December 1, 1908. Cf. the *Guardian*, July 28, 1909, p. 1188. According to the letter Petre sent to the *Guardian*, the Prior had told Tyrrell that his presence in the village of Storrington "was disagreeable and obnoxious to himself." And he had told Maude Petre to refuse Tyrrell admission to her house.

7. George Tyrrell had been excommunicated after two letters to the *Times* of London replying to the encyclical *Pascendi*. For a brief comment on the substance of the letters published September 30 and October 1, 1907, see Petre, *Autobiography and Life of George Tyrrell*, II, 337. A short chapter on the excommunication is to be found in the same volume, pp. 341–45.

8. British Museum, Add. MS. 52,374, Petre Papers, Vol. 8, Diary 3, February 13, 1909. For a discussion of the Marquise and of her sister, Baronness von Zedtwitz, and of their eventual conflict with Bishop Spalding, see, passim, David Sweeney, O.F.M., *The Life of John Lancaster Spalding* (New York: Herder and Herder, 1965).

9. British Museum, Add. MS. 52,374, Petre Papers, Vol. 8, Diary 3, February 26, 1909.

10. Petre, *Autobiography and Life of George Tyrrell*, II, 429.

11. Ibid., p. 423.

12. Ibid., pp. 425–26.

13. Ibid., p. 429. Dessoulavy (1875–1944) had been dismissed by Bishop Amigo as professor of philosophy at the Southwark diocesan seminary. See Vidler, *A Variety of Catholic Modernists*, p. 175.

14. Petre, *Autobiography and Life of George Tyrrell,* II, 431–32.

15. British Museum, Add. MS. 52,368, Petre Papers, Vol. 2. This material is in an account MDP kept of the death watch. Von Hügel reported in his diary, however, that Pollen saw Tyrrell alone. The Baron also disagreed with Petre's account in that he reported that Tyrrell was not lucid when he saw Dessoulavy. MDP had reported that Tyrrell spoke "long and consecutively." Dessoulavy wrote to von Hügel and substantiated the Baron's position on this. See de la Bedoyère, *The Life of Baron von Hügel* (London: J.M. Dent and Sons, 1952), pp. 232–33.

16. Petre, *Autobiography and Life of George Tyrrell,* II, 432.

17. See Vidler, *A Variety of Catholic Modernists,* p. 131. Next to nothing has been published about these intriguing women.

18. Lawrence Barmann also fills in a few details of Tyrrell's death-bed and funeral in his fine *Baron Friedrich von Hügel and the Modernist Crisis in England* (Cambridge: University Press, 1972), pp. 222–29.

19. British Museum, Add. MS. 52,374, Petre Papers, Vol. 8, Diary 3. Special four-page entry included after entry for August 5, 1909.

20. St. Andrew's University Library, Lilley Papers, Petre-Lilley, July 25, 1909.

21. Petre, *Autobiography and Life of George Tyrrell,* II, 434.

22. Ibid., pp. 434–35. For Loisy's account of the incidents surrounding Tyrrell's death, see his *Memoires,* III, 117.

23. British Museum, Add. MS. 52,368, Petre Papers, Vol. 2. This quotation as well as the description of the confusion surrounding Tyrrell's funeral and of the burial itself is taken from an account MDP wrote on the funeral of Tyrrell contained in this file at the British Museum as well as chapters 21 and 22 of the *Autobiography and Life of George Tyrrell.*

24. Petre, *Autobiography and Life of George Tyrrell,* II, 438.

25. Both this quotation and the evidence for the following paragraph in the text are taken from the funeral account MDP wrote and which was cited in note 23.

26. Ibid.

27. Petre, *Autobiography and Life of George Tyrrell,* II, 444. Bremond's funeral oration appears on pp. 442–44.

28. Reference again is made here to British Museum, Add. MS. 52, 368, Petre Papers, Vol. 2 and to MDP's account of the death-watch of Tyrrell contained therein. Italics are mine. On the question of Tyrrell's orthodoxy and the burial, Loisy wrote that neither Alfred Fawkes, nor von Hügel, nor Maude Petre contended that Tyrrell had died in official orthodoxy; rather, they insisted that he wished to die within the Roman

Catholic Communion. See Loisy's *Mémoires*, III, 128. In the same place, Loisy referred to Petre as a woman of intelligence and keen insight.

29. *Tablet* 82, (July 24, 1909), 130.

30. Ibid., July 31, 1909, p. 182.

31. Ibid., p. 181.

32. Maude Petre asked this question in a letter to the *Tablet* of August 28, 1909. She noted the letter again in the *Autobiography and Life of George Tyrrell*, II, 439.

Actually, in his refusal of burial, Bishop Amigo was probably working on the basis of the kind of procedure noted in standard moral theology manuals. A generation after the dispute over Tyrrell's death, for example, a standard manual of moral theology noted: "Neither may [an excommunicated person] receive any Sacrament nor (after a judicial sentence) a sacramental. He is likewise excluded from ecclesiastical burial (if a declaratory or condemnatory sentence has been passed). (c. 2260)." Herbert Jones, *Moral Theology* (Westminster, Md.: Newman Press, 1929).

33. *My Way of Faith*, pp. 267–68.

34. Ibid., p. 268.

35. Ibid., p. 269. It was about this same time that Bremond wrote to MDP about his own involvement in the Modernist movement: "I have given up the whole thing as hopeless long ago. I have no [sic] faith enough and I am too pessimistic to call myself a Modernist. . . ." British Museum, Add. MS. 52,380, Petre Papers, Vol. 14, Bremond-Petre, September 13, 1909.

36. See Petre, *Autobiography and Life of George Tyrrell*, II, 433: "I bequeath to Miss Maude Petre, of 16 Pitt Street, Kensington, London, W., all my manuscripts, copyrights, royalties and letters, and papers of literary interest, with full power to publish or destroy such letters or papers as she thinks fit. And I appoint her my Executor for such purpose. As witness my hand this 27th day of March 1905."

Gabriel Daly has expressed some dissatisfaction with some aspects of MDP's executorship. See his "Some Reflections on the Character of George Tyrrell," *Heythrop Journal* 10 (July 1969), 256–74. Speaking of problems involved in a study of Tyrrell, Daly noted: "There is one major critical problem which must be placed in evidence from the outset—the executive and editorial habits of Miss Maude Petre" (p. 256). Daly expressed appreciation for Petre's work on Tyrrell's *Autobiography*: "By any standards it is a striking piece of work, written with flawless taste and well documented with letters . . ." (pp. 256–57). But he noted: "Our worries begin with her honest admission, in the introduction to the first volume, that she has suppressed material which might be 'inconvenient' to the living. . . . It is not suppression, however, that is disturbing, but the destruction of original materials. One has no choice but to assume the loss of most of Tyrrell's letters to her. Some of those that have survived are cut" (pp. 257–58).

I can confirm that occasionally in the letters of Tyrrell to Petre in British Museum, Add. MS. 52,367, one comes across letters and notes that have been hacked off at the bottom. Maude Petre's diaries give evidence, too, that in the spring of 1920 she was disposing of some of the Tyrrell material. Thus, in March 1920, she reported, "Am going through G.T.'s papers and MSS destroying some, examining others—have destroyed the MS of the *Autobiography*." British Museum, Add. MS. 52,376, Petre Papers, Vol. 10, Diary 5, March 2, 1920. The following month she wrote: "Going through G.T.'s letters—burning many and leaving those that may remain." Ibid., April 19, 1920. And in May 1920 this entry appeared: ". . . reading through G.T.'s *Ethical Preludes* and destroyed part—more to be done." Ibid., May 17, 1920.

37. George Tyrrell, *Christianity at the Cross-Roads*, with an introduction by Maude Petre (London: Longmans, Green, 1909).

38. Maude Petre, "L'Evangile et L'Eglise d'après le P. Tyrrell," *Revue Moderniste Internationale* 1, No. 3 (1910), 89.

39. Petre, *Autobiography and Life of George Tyrrell*, II, 401.

40. Loisy, *Mémoires*, III, 128–36.

41. Ibid., p. 207.

6. The Cost of Allegiance

1. British Museum, Add. MS. 52,374, Petre Papers, Vol. 8, Diary 3, December 2, 1909.

2. St. Andrew's University Library, Lilley Papers, Petre-Lilley, December 10, 1909.

3. British Museum, Add. MS. 52,381, Petre Papers, Vol. 15, Amigo-Petre, December 7, 1909.

4. Ibid., Petre-Amigo, December 8, 1909. As is evident in this quotation, Maude Petre was not always technically scrupulous about underscoring titles. Her own usage will be continued in direct quotations from her throughout this study without further comment.

5. The bishop said in his letter, "The Fathers at Storrington make

the refusal of the Holy Communion to you a matter of conscience on the ground that you hold Modernist views condemned by the Encyclical *Pascendi*. If you assure me that their contention is wrong, I shall at once tell them to give you communion." Ibid., Amigo-Petre, December 10, 1909.

6. Mrs. Maurice Pirenne, Oxford, niece of Maude Petre, kindly showed me a copy of this family document and allowed me to copy it.

7. Maude Petre had consulted Baron von Hügel about her Easter Communion in 1910. She had thought about writing the bishop again, but von Hügel said that the bishop would "find some fresh demand or new alternative disadvantage," and that "every time you approach the Bishop you weaken that tactical strength." British Museum, Add. MS. 45,361, von Hügel-Petre, February 18, 1910.

8. British Museum, Add. MS. 52,381, Petre Papers, Vol. 15, Amigo-Petre, October 6, 1910.

9. Ibid., Petre-Amigo, October 6, 1910.

10. Ibid., Amigo-Petre, October 11, 1910.

11. Ibid., Petre-Amigo, October 14, 1910.

12. "Une Lettre ouverte de Miss Petre," 1, No. 11 (1910), 411.

13. "Per Il Pis pette del Santuario Della Coscienza," 4 (November 1910), 1–13. Miss Petre, the article said, was "pio virile di moltim uomini" (p. 1).

14. The anti-Modernist oath was imposed by the *Motu Proprio* "Sacrorum Antistitum" of Pius X, promulgated in September 1910, and very likely accounted in some manner for Bishop Amigo's extension of his discipline against MDP the following month. For the text of the papal letter, see *Acta Apostolicae Sedis* II (September 9, 1910), 655–80. An English translation of the oath is to be found in an appendix of Petre's *Modernism: Its Failure and Its Fruits* (London: T. C. and E. C. Jack, 1918), pp. 241–46.

15. Maude Petre, "An Open Letter to My Fellow Catholics," the *Times* (London), November 2, 1910, p. 6. Baron von Hügel with his customary diplomacy had urged MDP to write to the *Guardian* or the *Nation* rather than the *Times*. A letter to the *Times*, he feared, might cause Rome to pressure the Archbishop of Westminster to refuse her the sacraments in his diocese as well. British Museum, Add. MS. 45,362, von Hügel-Petre, October 24, 1910.

16. British Museum, Add. MS. 52,381, Petre Papers, Vol. 15, Doyle-Petre, November 6, 1910.

17. "A Regrettable Letter," *Tablet* 116 (November 5, 1910), 721–22.

18. Maude Petre, "Conscience and Subscription," *Tablet* 116 (November 12, 1910), 780.

19. Ibid., Editor's Note at conclusion of Petre's letter. The editor quoted the fourth chapter of the Dogmatic Constitution on Catholic Faith, *Dei Filius*, of the First Vatican Council: "Since it is not sufficient to shun heretical pravity, unless those errors also be avoided which more or less nearly approach it, we admonish all men of the further duty of observing those constitutions and decrees by which such erroneous opinions as are not here specifically enumerated, have been condemned and proscribed by this Holy See."

20. Antonia White, a British author who had known Maude Petre, wrote me the following in a letter of March 27, 1971: "[Maude Petre] came to London from Mulberry House, Storrington, because she was excommunicated in the diocese of Southwark, and so could not go to the sacraments in Sussex. But in London, in the diocese of Westminster, she could. [A priest] whom I know — a very holy man — said she used to go daily to the Carmelite Church in Kensington to Communion. He had the greatest respect for her and said she was a most holy and spiritual woman."

21. For an extensive accounting of MDP's sacramental difficulties, I refer the reader to my dissertation *The Role of Miss Maude Petre in the Modernist Movement* (Ann Arbor, Mich: University Microfilms, 1972), pp. 148–50. Some additional comments are to be found in Barmann, pp. 236–40.

22. Unfortunately no copy of the letter she sent the Vatican is among Petre's papers. There is, however, a letter in Italian from Cardinal Luigi Maglione, Pius XII's Secretary of State. The letter is dated April 14, 1939, and an English translation in what appears to be A. L. Lilley's handwriting is in the file at the British Museum: "Most Esteemed Lady — The Holy Father cannot but rejoice at the desire which is echoed in your Ladyship's letter. The Lord will dispose how and when he will be able to grant it. Meanwhile he entrusts it to Him with the most fervent prayer; and in sending to your Ladyship his paternal blessing he blesses also — invoking upon them light and teachableness of spirit — all who in sincerity of heart are straining towards one truth and are seeking it in charity." British Museum, Add. MS. 52,381, Petre Papers, Vol. 15, Maglione-Petre, April 14, 1939.

23. The writing must have taken up a good deal of time and energy. Petre did publish a very brief article in 1911 called "Réflexions

d'une Femme" that considered traits of the ideal priest — a man who remains a religious seeker. *Revue Moderniste Internationale* 2 (1911), 51–54.

24. Maude Petre's nephew, Sir George Clutton, who died in September 1970, had spoken with Bishop Amigo in April 1934 about his aunt. Bishop Amigo told Sir George that he had written the Sacred Congregation in Rome asking that they "allow the matter to die a natural death." Amigo feared that a condemnation would only increase sales of Tyrrell's *Autobiography and Life.* But in a secret letter of reply the Holy Office insisted that "measures must be taken against this 'sinful woman.' " Amigo declared that he thought Tyrrell to be an "unbalanced, untrustworthy and deceitful individual who had exerted a disastrous influence over his fellow creatures including Miss Petre." British Museum, Add. MS. 52,381, Petre Papers, Vol. 15, a written account of interview of Sir George Clutton with Bishop Amigo, April 1934.

25. Petre, *Autobiography and Life of George Tyrrell,* II, 58.

26. Ibid., pp. 219, 355.

27. Ibid., p. 383.

28. Ibid., pp. 335–36.

29. Ibid., pp. 449–50.

30. British Museum, Add. MS. 52,374, Petre Papers, Vol. 8, Diary 3, November 26, 1909. Miss Petre had consulted Bremond in what must have been the very early stages of the project. "Bremond thinks, with me, it will be one of the world's greatest autobiographies — greater than Newman's, than St. Augustine's!"

31. "Autobiography and Life of George Tyrrell," *America* 8 (November 30, 1912), 187–88.

32. Petre, *Autobiography and Life of George Tyrrell,* II, 374.

33. Alfred Fawkes, "Autobiography and Life," *Quarterly Review* (January 1913), 71. Fawkes also noted: "Miss Petre has said out all that there is to say with a frankness as honorable to herself as it is just to the distinguished man who, knowing where confidence was well bestowed, left his memory in her keeping. The trust has been discharged in the face of obstacles which might have daunted a less fine spirit; the terrors of the next world were called in to supplement the weapons of this; both were invoked in vain."

34. George Tyrrell, *Essays on Faith and Immortality* (London: T. Fisher Unwin, 1919).

35. Maude Petre, ed., *George Tyrrell's Letters* (London: T. Fisher Unwin, 1920).

36. Vidler, *The Modernist Movement in the Roman Church*, p. 204.

37. Petre, *Modernism: Its Failure and Its Fruits*, p. 3.

7. War and Peace

1. See Paul Fussell's fine work *The Great War and Modern Memory* (Princeton: University Press, 1975).

2. Loisy, *Memoires*, III, 172.

3. British Museum, Add. MS. 52,375, Petre Papers, Vol. 9, Diary 4, September 20, 1914.

4. "The Advantages and Disadvantages of Authority in Religion," *Hibbert Journal* 12 (January 1914), 303.

5. Ibid., p. 295.

6. Ibid., p. 300.

7. British Museum, Add. MS. 52,375, Petre Papers, Vol. 9, Diary 4, September 30, 1914.

8. *Times*, October 26, 1914.

9. British Museum, Add. MS. 52,375, Petre Papers, Vol. 9, Diary 4, March 24, 1915.

10. Ibid., May 8, 10, 1915.

11. Ibid., May 9, 1916.

12. *Reflections of a Non-Combatant* (London: Longmans, Green, 1915), p. v.

13. *Catholic World* 102 (January 1916), 549.

14. *My Way of Faith*, p. 302.

15. Ibid., pp. 303–4.

16. Ibid., p. 307.

17. Ibid., p. 304.

18. "Christianity and War," *Edinburgh Review* 222 (October 1915), 298.

19. Ibid., p. 305.

20. Ibid., pp. 327–28.

21. "Religion and Patriotism," *Edinburgh Review* 228 (October 1918), 328.

22. Maude Petre, *Democracy at the Cross-Roads* (London: T. Fisher Unwin, 1918), p. 124. An appreciative review was carried in the *Quarterly Review* 231 (April 1919), 517–18.

23. *My Way of Faith*, p. 299.

24. Petre, *Democracy at the Cross-Roads*, p. 54.

25. Ibid., pp. 83-84.

26. Maude Petre and James A. Walker, *State Morality and a League of Nations* (London: T. Fisher Unwin, 1919).

27. Ibid., p. 83.

28. Ibid., p. 100.

29. "The City on Earth, the City in Heaven and the League of Nations," *Hibbert Journal* 18 (April 1920), 469. MDP also wrote a letter opposing national selfishness titled "The Labour Party and International Warfare" in *The Nation* 28 (October 30, 1920), 163-65.

30. Pierre Teilhard de Chardin, *Building the Earth* (Wilkes-Barre, Pa.: Dimension, 1965), pp. 19-40.

31. *The Fascist Movement in Italian Life*, trans. Maude Petre (London: T. Fisher Unwin, 1923).

32. Ibid., p. 10.

33. Ibid., pp. 19-20. Maude Petre was fully aware of the dangers and evils of fascism. She spoke of it as in some ways being "the definite negation of liberty." See Maude Petre, "Fascism and Its Relation to Freedom," *Nineteenth Century* 202 (October 1927), 490.

34. *The Two Cities* (London: Longmans, Green, 1925), p. 24.

35. Ibid.

36. Ibid., pp. 26-27.

37. Ibid.

38. Ibid., pp. 27-28.

39. Ibid., pp. 95-96.

40. Ibid., p. 99.

41. "Bolshevist Ideals and the 'Brave New World,'" *Hibbert Journal* 31 (October 1932), 63. MDP compressed her thought on bolshevism and Christianity in a letter: "Bolshevik Mentality," *Dublin Review* 188 (April 1931), 313-15.

42. *Hibbert Journal* 40 (January 1942), 118.

43. Ibid., pp. 121-22.

44. Ibid., p. 124.

45. Petre, "Nationalism and Christianity: Can Christianity Save the World?" *Adelphi*, July 1939.

46. Ibid., p. 7.

47. Ibid., p. 8.

48. Ibid., p. 10.

49. Ibid., p. 32.

8. Modernism's Early Historian

1. Maude Petre, *Modernism: Its Failure and Its Fruits*, p. v.
2. Ibid., p. 1.
3. Ibid.
4. Ibid., pp. 2–3.
5. Ibid., p. 3.
6. Ibid., p. 12.
7. Ibid., p. 23.
8. Ibid., p. 33.
9. Ibid., p. 40.
10. Ibid., pp. 40–41.
11. Ibid., p. 42.
12. Ibid., pp. 50–51.
13. Ibid., p. 54.
14. Ibid., p. 59.
15. Ibid., p. 60.
16. Ibid., p. 63.
17. Ibid., p. 56.
18. Ibid., p. 71.
19. Ibid., p. 83.
20. Ibid., pp. 85–86.
21. Ibid., pp. 86–87.
22. Ibid., p. 89.
23. Ibid., p. 88.
24. Ibid., p. 90.
25. Ibid., pp. 92–93.
26. Ibid., p. 94.
27. Ibid.
28. Ibid., p. 95.
29. Ibid., p. 97.
30. Ibid., p. 98.
31. Ibid., p. 106.
32. Ibid., p. 107.
33. Ibid., p. 108.
34. Ibid., pp. 114–15.
35. Ibid., p. 115.
36. Ibid., p. 116.
37. Ibid., p. 141.
38. Ibid., p. 150.

39. Ibid., p. 153.

40. Ibid., p. 140.

41. Ibid., p. 154.

42. "A Religious Movement of the First Years of Our Century," *Horizon* 6 (November 1942), 329–30.

43. *Modernism: Its Failure and Its Fruits*, p. 148.

44. Bibliotheque Nationale, N.A.F. 15,660, Loisy Papers, Vol. 27, pp. 121–22. Petre-Loisy, August 23, 1931.

45. *Modernism: Its Failure and Its Fruits*, p. 179.

46. Ibid., p. 180.

47. Ibid.

48. Ibid., p. 181.

49. Ibid., p. 182.

50. Ibid., p. 183.

51. Ibid., p. 3.

52. Ibid., p. 201.

53. Ibid., p. 203.

54. Ibid., p. 209.

55. Ibid., p. 207.

56. Ibid.

57. Ibid., p. 213.

58. Ibid., pp. 216–17. An unfavorable review of Maude Petre's history by Josephine Ward is to be found as an appendix in Maisie Ward's *Insurrection versus Resurrection* (New York: Sheed and Ward, 1937), pp. 553–58.

9. "After All Our Hopes"

1. *My Way of Faith*, pp. 239–40.

2. British Museum, Add. MS. 52,377, Petre Papers, Vol. 11, Diary 6, April 16, 1933.

3. *My Way of Faith*, p. 210.

4. Ibid., pp. 243–44.

5. Ibid., p. 241.

6. *Von Hügel and Tyrrell: The Story of a Friendship* (London: J. M. Dent and Sons, 1937), p. 9.

7. Ibid., p. 199.

8. *Alfred Loisy: His Religious Significance* (Cambridge: University Press, 1944), p. 33.

9. "Divine and Human Faith," *Nineteenth Century* 84 (October 1918), 655.

10. Ibid.

11. Ibid., p. 658.

12. Ibid., p. 657.

13. "The Moral Factor in Society," *Modern Churchman* 13 (June 1924), 120–21. Still, there were times when MDP herself leaned toward at least a modified symbolism. Consider this item from "George Tyrrell and Friedrich von Hügel in Their Relation to Catholic Modernism," *Modern Churchman* 17 (June 1927), 146: "The Church knew instinctively that there were elements of her doctrine which would not bear the test of criticism, because they were not intended to bear that test; she had a subconscious, though certainly not a conscious, sense of the relativity, the temporal limitations, the symbolism of her own teaching."

14. British Museum, Add. MS. 52,379, Petre Papers, Vol. 13, Diary 8, May 26, 1938.

15. Alec Vidler, *Twentieth Century Defenders of the Faith* (London: SCM, 1965), p. 109.

16. *Alfred Loisy: His Religious Significance*, p. 98.

17. Ibid., p. 8.

18. Ibid., p. 21.

19. Ibid.

20. Robert Graves and Alan Hodge, *The Long Week-End: A Social History of Great Britain, 1918-1939.* (New York: Macmillan, 1940).

21. "The Creative Elements of Tyrrell's Religious Thought," *Modern Churchman* 18 (March 1929), 701.

22. Ibid.

23. *George Tyrrell's Letters*, pp. xvi–xvii.

24. "A Religious Movement of the First Years of Our Century," *Horizon* 6 (November 1942), 338.

25. *My Way of Faith*, p. xxv.

26. "An Open Letter to Lord Halifax," *The Guardian*, June 8, 1923.

27. "The Church in Its Relation to Religion," *Modern Churchman* 13 (September 1923), 290.

28. *My Way of Faith*, p. 236.

29. "The Church in Its Relation to Religion," p. 289.

30. "Still At It: The Impasse of Modern Christology," *Hibbert Journal* 20 (April 1922), 407.

31. "Cristo Nella Chiesa Cattolica," *Ricerche Religiose* 4 (1928), 447–49.

32. *My Way of Faith*, p. 214.

33. Ibid., p. 212.

34. Ibid., p. 98.

35. *The Ninth Lord Petre*, p. 325.

36. See above, chapter 1.

37. *The Ninth Lord Petre*, p. 323.

38. *My Way of Faith*, p. 233.

39. Ibid., pp. 341–42. Reviews of *My Way of Faith* which concluded with the Catholic apologia were mixed. The Jesuit weekly *America* headlined its review by R. J. McInnis: "Prefers Tyrrell to Holy Father" (July 31, 1937); *Commonweal's* Paul Crowley considered that some passages "belong in the company of treasured excerpts from religious literature" (June 4, 1937). J. McSorley of the *Catholic World* noted that "one finds it difficult to criticize a person so obviously spiritual, honest, courageous and loyal as Maude Petre" (August 1937).

40. Diary 8, October 5, 1938.

41. Mrs. Cally Merewether made these remarks to the present writer in an interview in London on November 22, 1970.

42. Mrs. Merewether in same interview as that above.

43. Diary 8, June 27, 1941.

44. Ibid., October 1, 1942 and subsequent October references.

45. Ibid., December 11, 1942.

46. James Walker, "Maude Petre: A Memorial Tribute," p. 340.

47. Ibid.

48. London *Times*, December 19, 1942. MDP's "death card" bore a quotation from the *Imitation of Christ*, II, 8: "After the winter cometh summer, after the night, the day returneth, after the storm cometh a great calm."

49. Walker, p. 340.

50. Interview of Sir George Clutton with Bishop Peter Amigo, April 1943. British Museum, Add. MS. 52,381, Petre Papers, Vol. 15.

51. Walker, p. 341. Walker said of Maude Petre: "There was no good cause in Sussex that she had not served zealously. She had been chairman of Storrington Parish Council for several years, the life and soul of the Woman's Institute, the pioneer of the local housing scheme, the founder of a Cottage Hospital."

52. *My Way of Faith*, p. 342.

53. Walker, p. 341.

54. British Museum, Add. MS. 52,381, Lilley-Walker, n.d.

10. Conclusion

1. With two exceptions, all quotations in this conclusion have already been cited throughout the study, and will not be noted here again.

2. *My Way of Faith*, p. 235.

3. Petre, "George Tyrrell and Friedrich von Hügel in Their Relation to Catholic Modernism," p. 154.

Selected Bibliography

I. Manuscript Collections

Bibliotheque Nationale (Paris). N.A.F. 15,660. Loisy Papers, Vol. 27, pp. 1–270.

British Museum. Add. MSS. 44,927–44,931. Von Hügel-Tyrrell Correspondence.

_____. Add. MSS. 45,361–45,362. Von Hügel-Petre Correspondence.

_____. Add. MSS. 45,744–45,745. Letters to Maude Petre from various correspondents.

_____. Add. MSS. 52,367–52,382. The Petre Papers, 16 vols.:

Vol. 1. Add. MS. 52,367. Letters of George Tyrrell to Maude Petre (1898–1908).

Vol. 2. Add. MS. 52,368. Letters of George Tyrrell to his Jesuit Superiors (1901–1906); George Tyrrell Correspondence (1900–1908); Material re: Tyrrell's Death (1909–1933).

Vol. 3. Add. MS. 52,369. Writings of George Tyrrell—

A. "Revelation as Experience"—a reply to Hakluyt Egerton: King's College Hostel, London (1909);

B. "Beati Excommunicati" (1904), published as "L'Excommunication Salutaire," in *La Grande Revue* 64 (October 1907), 661–72.

Vols. 4–5. Add. MSS. 52,370–52,371. *Christianity at the Cross-Roads.*

Vols. 6–8. Add. MSS. 52,372–52,379. Maude Petre Diaries—

A. Vol. 6. Add. MS. 52,372. Diary 1 (1900–1902).

B. Vol. 7. Add. MS. 52,373. Diary 2 (1902–1906).

C. Vol. 8. Add. MS. 52,374. Diary 3 (1906–1910).

D. Vol. 9. Add. MS. 52,375. Diary 4 (1910–1918).

E. Vol. 10. Add. MS. 52,376. Diary 5 (1918–1926).

F. Vol. 11. Add. MS. 52,377. Diary 6 (1929–1933).

G. Vol. 12. Add. MS. 52,378. Diary 7 (1933–1937).

H. Vol. 13. Add. MS. 52,379. Diary 8 (1937–1942).

Vol. 14. Add. MS. 52,380. Letters of Henri Bremond to Maude Petre (1900–1935).

Vol. 15. Add. MS. 52,381. General Correspondence of Maude Petre; also Correspondence of Maude Petre's literary executor, James A. Walker.

Vol. 16. Add. MS. 52,382. Four Drawings for the *Autobiography and Life of George Tyrrell.*

Cambridge University Library. The Anderson Room. Five Scrapbooks on George Tyrrell compiled by Maude Petre.

St. Andrews University Library (Scotland). Lilley Papers. Petre-Lilley Correspondence.

II. Published Writings of Maude Petre*

A. Books

Aethiopum Servus: A Study in Christian Altruism. London: Osgood, McIlvane, 1896.
> Review: "Life of Peter Claver and Work with Slaves." *Catholic World* 62 (March 1896), 846.

Where Saints Have Trod: Some Studies in Asceticism. London: Catholic Truth Society, 1903.
> Reviews: *Catholic World* 79 (August 1904), 683–84.
> *Dublin Review* 135 (October 1904), 431–33.

The Temperament of Doubt. London: Catholic Truth Society, 1903.

Devotional Essays. London: Catholic Truth Society, 1904.

Catholicism and Independence: Being Studies in Spiritual Liberty. London: Longmans, Green, 1907.

Reflections of a Non-Combatant. London: Longmans, Green, 1915.
> Review: *Catholic World* 102 (January 1916), 549.

Autobiography and Life of George Tyrrell. 2 vols. New York: Longmans, Green, 1912.

---

* Throughout the bibliography of the published writings of Maude Petre, the style of chronological sequence will be employed. Some of the reviews of the longer works are noted directly beneath these works.

Reviews: *America* 8 (November 30, 1912), 187–88.

        Fawkes, Alfred. *Quarterly Review* 218 (January 1913), 71–90.

Democracy at the Cross-Roads. London: T. Fisher Unwin, 1918.

Review: *Quarterly Review* 231 (April 1919), 517–18.

Modernism: Its Failure and Its Fruits. London: T. C. and E. C. Jack, 1918.

The Two Cities or Statecraft and Idealism. London: Longmans, Green, 1925.

The Ninth Lord Petre: Pioneers of Roman Catholic Emancipation. London: SPCK, 1928.

Reviews: *America* 39 (May 26, 1928), 165.

        Commonweal 8 (October 31, 1928), 671.

My Way of Faith. London: J. M. Dent and Sons, 1937.

Reviews: Crowley, Paul. "Spiritual Quest." *Commonweal* 26 (June 4, 1937), 166.

        Gaul, Cecelia. *Christian Century* 54 (September 8, 1937), 1109.

        Lilley, A. L. "Miss M. D. Petre's *Apologia.*" *Modern Churchman* 27 (July 1937), 207–10.

        _____. *Journal of Theological Studies* 40 (1939), 91–94.

        McGarry, W. J., S.J. *Thought* 12 (December 1937), 683.

        McInnis, R. J., S.J. "Prefers Tyrrell to Holy Father." *America* 57 (July 31, 1937), 195.

        McSorley, J., C.S.P. *Catholic World* 145 (August 1937), 630–31.

        Manson, Aelfric, O.P. *Blackfriars* 18 (April 1937), 312–13.

Von Hügel and Tyrrell: The Story of a Friendship. London: J. M. Dent and Sons, 1937.

Review: *Commonweal* 28 (July 29, 1938), 372.

        Webb, Clement C. J. "Von Hügel and Tyrrell." *Journal of Theological Studies* 39 (April 1938), 214–17.

Alfred Loisy: His Religious Significance. With an Introduction, "Maude Petre," by James A. Walker. Cambridge: University Press, 1944.

Reviews: Cotter, A. C., S.J. *Theological Studies* 6 (March 1945), 129.

        Lilley, A. L. *Journal of Theological Studies* 40 (1944), 237.

B. Articles and Essays

"Victor Hugo." *Month* 54 (July 1885), 318–30.

"Carlyle on Religious Ceremonies." *Month* 55 (November 1885), 314–21.

"Shades of the Prison House." *Month* 93 (April 1899), 381–89.

"Lawful Liberty and Reasonable Service." *American Catholic Quarterly Review* 24 (July 1899), 90–101.

"Stray Thoughts on the Woman's International Congress." *Month* 94 (August 1899), 186–93.

"The White-Robed Army." *Month* 96 (September 1900), 225–32.

"An Englishwoman's Love Letters." *Month* 97 (February 1901), 116–26.

"Devotion and Devotions." *Weekly Register*. A three-part series: November 22, 1901, pp. 635–36; November 29, 1901, pp. 669–70; December 6, 1901, pp. 701–2.

"Alma Mater." *Weekly Register*, March 14, 1902, p. 317.

"The Order of Melchisidek." *Monthly Register*, 1902, pp. 265–67.

"Unum Necessarium." *Monthly Register*, 1902, pp. 224–26.

"Human Love and Divine Love." *Catholic World* 74 (January 1902), 442–53.

"De Profundis." *Month* 105 (April 1905), 383–87.

"Pessimism in Its Relation to Asceticism." *Catholic World* 81 (April 1905), 33–43.

"Studies on Friedrich Nietzsche." *Catholic World*. A six-part series:
"A Life Militant." 82 (December 1905), 317–30.
"Nietzsche: The Poet." 82 (January 1906), 516–26.
"Nietzsche: The Anti-Moralist." 82 (February 1906), 610–21.
"The Superman." 82 (March 1906), 777–84.
"Nietzsche: The Anti-Feminist." 83 (May 1906), 159–70.
"Nietzsche: The Anti-Christian." 83 (June 1906), 345–55.

"Il Santo and Another Saint." *Commonwealth* 11 (February 1906), 166–68.

"The Fallacy of Undenominationalism." *Catholic World* 84 (February 1907), 640–46.

"Una Nuova Apologia Cattolica." *Il Rinnovamento* 1 (May 1907), 567–76.

"Ossequio o Idolatria?" *Nova et Vetera* 2 (October 1908), 205–10.

Letter to the Editor. *Times* (London), July 16, 1909, p. 13.

Letter to the Editor. *Guardian*, July 28, 1909, p. 1185. This and the following two letters dealt with Tyrrell's death.

Letter to the Editor. *Tablet* 114 (July 31, 1909), 181.

Letter to the Editor. *Times* (London), July 31, 1909, p. 10.

"An Open Letter to My Fellow Catholics." *Times* (London), November 2, 1910, p. 6.

"Conscience and Subscription." *Tablet* 116 (November 12, 1910).

"Per Il Pispetto del Santuario Della Coscienza." *Coenobium* 4 (November 1910), 1–13.

"L'Evangile et L'Eglise d'après le P. Tyrrell." *Revue Moderniste Internationale* 1, No. 3 (1910), 89–91.

"Une Lettre ouverte de Miss Petre." *Revue Moderniste Internationale* 1, No. 11 (1910), 411–14; and 1, No. 12 (1910), 447–50.

"Reflexions d'une Femme." *Revue Moderniste Internationale* 2, No. 2 (1911), 51–54.

"The Woman's Movement: Neglected Opportunities." *Times* (London), October 29, 1913, p. 13.

"The Advantages and Disadvantages of Authority in Religion." *Hibbert Journal* 12 (January 1914), 295–305.

"Let Us Be English." *Times* (London), October 26, 1914.

"Christianity and War." *Edinburgh Review* 222 (October 1915), 294–311.

"Machiavelli and Modern Statecraft." *Edinburgh Review* 226 (July 1917), 93–112.

"He That Loveth His Life Shall Lose It." *The Free Catholic* (1917), pp. 22–27.

"Divine and Human Faith." *Nineteenth Century* 84 (October 1918), 642–59.

"Religion and Patriotism." *Edinburgh Review* 228 (October 1918), 313–30.

"The City on Earth, the City in Heaven and the League of Nations." *Hibbert Journal* 18 (April 1920), 459–69.

"The Labour Party and International Welfare." *Nation* (London) 28 (October 30, 1920), 163–65.

"Still At It: The Impasse of Modern Christology." *Hibbert Journal* 20 (April 1922), 401–10.

"An Open Letter to Lord Halifax." *Guardian*, June 8, 1923.

"The Roman Catholic Church and Reunion." *Modern Churchman* 13 (April 1923), 14–20.

"Religious Authority." *Modern Churchman* 13 (July 1923), 176–85.

"The Church in Its Relation to Religion." *Modern Churchman* 13 (September 1923), 288–93.

"The Moral Factor in Society." *Modern Churchman* 13 (June 1924), 114–21.

"Friedrich von Hügel: Personal Thoughts and Reminiscences." *Hibbert Journal* 24 (October 1925), 77–87.

"An Deus Sit?" *Hibbert Journal* 24 (April 1926), 397–403.

"George Tyrrell and Friedrich von Hügel in Their Relation to Catholic Modernism." *Modern Churchman* 17 (June 1927), 143–54.

"Fascism and Its Relation to Freedom." *Nineteenth Century* 202 (October 1927), 479–93.

"Cristo Nella Chiesa Cattolica." *Ricerche Religiose* 4 (1928), 447–49.

"The Creative Elements of Tyrrell's Religious Thought." *Modern Churchman* 18 (March 1929), 695–703.

"Poetry and Prayer." *Dublin Review* 185 (October 1929), 177–93.

"Il Destino di Lamennais." *Ricerche Religiose* 5 (1929), 538–44.

"La Catastrophe di Lamennais." *Ricerche Religiose* 6 (1930), 502–18.

"L'Ultramontanismo di Lamennais." *Ricerche Religiose* 6 (1930), 333–45.

"La Religione di Lamennais." *Ricerche Religiose* 7 (1931), 133–45.

"La Filosofia dell'uomo e di Dio in Lamennais." *Ricerche Religiose* 8 (1932), 144–54.

"Some Thoughts on the Career of Feli de Lamennais." *Modern Churchman* 19 (January 1930), 592–98. A translation of "Felice di Lamennais."

"Feli de Lamennais II: Essai sur l'Indifférence." *Modern Churchman* 19 (February 1930), 641–53. A translation of "Il Destino di Lamennais."

"George Tyrrell and Alfred Fawkes." *Modern Churchman* 20 (1930), 542–43.

"Ignorance and Wisdom." *Dublin Review* 188 (January 1931), 97–107.

"Bolshevik Mentality." *Dublin Review* 188 (April 1931), 313–15.

"M. Loisy's Autobiography." *Hibbert Journal* 29 (July 1931), 655–66.

"Von Hugel and the Great Quest." *Modern Churchman* 21 (1931), 475–83.

"La Filosofia del Male nel 'Paradiso Perdito.'" *Ricerche Religiose* 8 (1932), 409–15.

Letter to the Editor. *Times* (London), July 24, 1932. The subject was the disposition of George Tyrrell at his death.

"New Wine in Old Bottles." *Modern Churchman* 22 (July 1932), 212–18.

"Bolshevist Ideas and the 'Brave New World.'" *Hibbert Journal* 31 (October 1932), 61–71.

"Père Laberthonnière." *Hibbert Journal* 31 (April 1933), 417–26.

"The Religious Philosophy of Baron von Hügel." *Adelphi* VI, No. 3 (1933), 229–30.

"Some Reflections on D. H. Lawrence from the Catholic Point of View." *Adelphi* VI, No. 5 (1933), 337–45.

"Poetry and Intelligibility." *Blackfriars* 15 (October 1934), 660–70.

With H. F. Stewart. "Babel and Anti-Babel." *Spectator* 158 (January 1937), 173.

With H. F. Stewart. "Anti-Babel Society." *Spectator* 160 (June 1938), 1101.

"Comment on M. Loisy's Articles." *Hibbert Journal* 36 (July 1938), 530–33.

"Parliament and Peace." *Adelphi* 15, No. 10 (1938), 86–88.

"Symposium on Professor J. MacMurray's *Clue to History.*" *Adelphi* 16, No. 5 (1939), 231–32.

"Nationalism and Christianity: Can Christianity Save the World?" *Adelphi* 16, No. 10 (1939), a supplement, 1–32.

"Paul Desjardins: Personal Reminiscences." *Hibbert Journal* 38 (July 1940), 505–10.

"Alfred Loisy." *Theology* 41 (September 1940), 132–40.

"Alfred Loisy." *Hibbert Journal* 39 (October 1940), 5–14. This article is not identical to the preceding one.

"The Individual and the Collective." *Adelphi* 17, No. 4 (1941), 102–8.

"What Russia Can Teach Us." *Hibbert Journal* 40 (January 1942), 113–24.

"Property and Possession." *Hibbert Journal* 41 (October 1942), 60–67.

"A Religious Movement of the First Years of Our Century." *Horizon* 6 (November 1942), 328–42.

C. Short Reviews by Maude Petre

Review of *Weltkirche und Weltfriede* by Franziskus Stratman, O.P. *Dublin Review* 177 (July 1925), 135–38.

Review of *La Consolation d'Israel* by Alfred Loisy. *Hibbert Journal* 26 (October 1927), 181–85.

Review of *Pages Choisies* by Alfred Loisy. *Dublin Review* 188 (April 1931), 348–50.

"Emmanuel Swedenborg: The True Christian Religion." *Adelphi* 6, No. 3 (1933), 232–33.

Review of *Autres Mythes à propos de la Religion* by Alfred Loisy. *Hibbert Journal* 37 (January 1939), 344–46.

Review of *Selected Mystical Writings of William Law*. *Journal of Theological Studies* 11 (1939), 309–10.

Review of *Un Mythe Apologétique* by Alfred Loisy. *Journal of Theological Studies* 11 (1940), 340–41.

D. Editings, Translations, Collaborations

The Soul's Orbit or Man's Journey to God. London: Longmans, Green, 1904. Compiled by Maude Petre, who was partial author. The major part of the book was, however, the work of Tyrrell.
    Reviews: *American Ecclesiastical Review* 32 (February 1905), 196–98.
        Catholic World 80 (January 1905), 550–52.
        Dublin Review 137 (October 1905), 401.

Tyrrell, George. *Christianity at the Cross-Roads*. Edited by Maude Petre with an introduction. London: Longmans, Green, 1909.
    Review: *Church Times*, November 5, 1909, p. 603.

_____. *Essays on Faith and Immortality*. Arranged by Maude Petre with an Introduction. London: E. Arnold, 1914.

_____. *George Tyrrell's Letters*. Edited by Maude Petre with an Introduction. London: T. Fisher Unwin, 1920.

Petre, Maude, and James A. Walker. *State Morality and A League of Nations*. London: T. Fisher Unwin, 1919.

Nietzsche, Friedrich. *The Joyful Wisdom*. Translated by Thomas Common with poetry rendered by Paul Cohn and Maude Petre. London: T. N. Foulis, 1918.

Gorgolini, Pietro. *The Fascist Movement in Italian Life*. Translated by Maude Petre, with an Introduction by Benito Mussolini. London: T.Fisher Unwin, 1923.

III. Modernist-Related Sources

Aubert, Roger. "The Modernist Crisis." In Hubert Jedin and John Dolan, eds., *The Church in the Industrial Age*, pp. 420–80. New York: Crossroad, 1981.

_____. "The Modernist Crisis and the Integrist Reaction." In Aubert et al., *The Church in a Secularized Society*. New York: Paulist Press, 1978.

_____. "Recent Literature on the Modernist Movement." In *Concilium*, Vol. 18: 91–108. Glen Rock, N.J.: Paulist Press, 1969.

Barmann, Lawrence. *Baron Friedrich von Hügel and the Modernist Crisis in England.* Cambridge: University Press, 1972.

Blondel, Maurice. *The Letter on Apologetics and History and Dogma.* Edited and translated by Alexander Dru and Illtyd Trethowan. New York: Holt, Rinehart and Winston, 1964.

Bouillard, Henri. *Blondel and Christianity.* Washington: Corpus Books, 1969.

Burke, Ronald, and George Gilmore, eds. *Current Research in Roman Catholic Modernism.* Spring Hill, Ala.: College Press, 1980.

Daly, Gabriel. "Some Reflections on the Career of George Tyrrell." *Heythrop Journal* 10 (July 1969), 265–74.

———. *Transcendence and Immanence: A Study in Catholic Modernism and Integralism.* Oxford: Clarendon Press, 1980.

Daniel-Rops, Henri. *A Fight for God.* London: J. M. Dent and Sons, 1966.

Hamilton, Robert. "Faith and Knowledge: The Autobiography of Maude Petre." *Downside Review* 85 (April 1967), 148–59.

Heaney, John J. *The Modernist Crisis: von Hügel.* Washington: Corpus Books, 1968.

Houtin, Albert, *Histoire du Modernisme Catholique.* Paris: Chez l'auteur, 1913.

Hügel, Friedrich von. Letter to the Editor. *Tablet* 114 (July 31, 1909), 181–82. The letter concerns Tyrrell's death.

Kelly, J. J. "The Modernist Controversy: von Hügel and Blondel." *Ephemerides Theologicae Lovanienses* 55 (December 1979), 297–330.

La Bedoyère, Michael de. *The Life of Baron von Hügel.* London: J. M. Dent and Sons, 1952.

Leonard, Ellen. *George Tyrrell and the Catholic Tradition.* New York: Paulist Press, 1982.

Lilley, A. L. *Modernism: A Record and a Review.* New York: Scribner's, 1908.

Loisy, Alfred. *Autour d'un petit livre.* Paris: Alphonse Picard, 1903.

———. *The Gospel and the Church.* New York: Scribner's, 1904. New edition edited by Bernard Brandon Scott: Philadelphia, Fortress Press, 1976.

———. *Mémoires pour servir à l'histoire religieuse de nôtre temps.* 3 vols. Paris: Nourry, 1931.

Loome, Thomas. *Liberal Catholicism, Reform Catholicism, Catholic Modernism.* Mainz: Matthias-Grunewald, 1979.

Louis-David, Anne. "The Latest from Mudie's" *Month* 2nd n.s. 1 (May 1970), 294–302.

———. ed. *George Tyrrell: Lettres à Henri Bremond.* Paris: Aubier Montaigne, 1971.

May, James Lewis. *Father Tyrrell and the Modernist Movement.* London: Eyre and Spottiswoode, 1932.

Nédoncelle, Maurice. *La pensée religieuse de Friedrich von Hügel 1852–1925.* Paris: Vrin, 1935.

Nelson, Claud, and Norman Pittenger, eds. *Pilgrim of Rome: Introduction to the Life and Work of Ernesto Buonaiuti.* London: Nisbit, 1970.

Pius X. *Lamentabili. Acta Sanctae Sedis.* Rome: Typographia Polyglotta. S. Cong. de Propaganda Fide, 1907, pp. 469–78. English translation in pamphlet *Pascendi.* Washington: N.C.W.C., 1963, pp. 45–50.

———. *Pascendi. Acta Sanctae Sedis.* Rome: Typographia Polyglotta. S. Cong. de Propaganda Fide, 1907, pp. 593–650. English translation in pamphlet *Pascendi.* Washington: N.C.W.C., 1963, pp. 1–44.

———. *Sacrorum Antistitum. Acta Apostolicae Sedis*, II (September 9, 1910), 655–80.

Poulat, Emile. *Histoire, dogme et critique dans la Crise Moderniste.* Paris: Casterman, 1962.

Rahner, Karl, and Herbert Vorgrimler. "Modernism." In *Theological Dictionary.* New York: Herder and Herder, 1967.

Ranchetti, Michele. *The Catholic Modernists 1864–1907.* Oxford: University Press, 1970.

Ratté, John. "Church, Modernism in the Christian." In *Dictionary of the History of Ideas* I, 418–27. New York: Scribner's, 1973.

———. *Three Modernists.* New York: Sheed and Ward, 1967.

Reardon, Bernard, ed. *Roman Catholic Modernism.* London: Adam and Charles Black, 1970.

"A Regrettable Letter." *Tablet* 116 (November 5, 1910), 721–22.

Rivière, Jean. *Le Modernisme dans l'Eglise.* Paris: Letouzey et Ané, 1929.

Root, John. "English Catholic Modernism and Science." *Heythrop Journal* 18 (July 1977), 271–88.

Schultenover, David, S.J. *George Tyrrell: In Search of Catholicism.* Shepherdstown, W. Va.: Patmos Press, 1981.

Scoppola, Pietro. *Crisi modernista e rinnovamento cattolico in Italia.* Bologna: Il Mulino, 1961.

Smith, E. Harold. Introduction to the new edition of Alfred Loisy's *My Duel with the Vatican.* Translated by Richard Boynton. New York: Greenwood, 1968.

Snape, H. C. "Portrait of a Devout Humanist." *Harvard Theological Review* 97 (January 1954), 15–53.

Somerville, James. *Total Commitment*. Washington: Corpus Books, 1968.

Steinmann, Jean. *Friedrich von Hügel: sa vie, son oeuvre, ses amitiés*. Paris: Aubier, 1962.

Trevor, Meriol. *Prophets and Guardians*. Garden City, N.Y.: Doubleday, 1969.

Tyrrell, George. *A Much-Abused Letter*. London: Longmans, Green, 1906.

_____. "A Perverted Devotion." *Weekly Register*, December 16, 1899, pp. 797–800.

_____. *Through Scylla and Charybdis*. London: Longmans, Green, 1907.

Vidler, Alec. *The Modernist Movement in the Roman Church*. Cambridge: University Press, 1934.

_____. *Twentieth Century Defenders of the Faith*. London: S.C.M., 1965.

_____. *A Variety of Catholic Modernists*. Cambridge: University Press, 1970.

Xavier, F., C.R.P. Letter to the Editor. *Tablet* 114 (July 24, 1909), 130–31. The Prior of Storrington commenting on Tyrrell's death.

Walker, James A. "Maude Petre." Introduction to Maude Petre's *Alfred Loisy: His Religious Significance*, pp. vii–xi. Cambridge: University Press, 1944.

_____. "Maude Petre: A Memorial Tribute." *Hibbert Journal* 41 (April 1943), 340–46.

Weaver, Mary Jo, ed. *Letters from a "Modernist": The Letters of George Tyrrell to Wilfrid Ward*. Shepherdstown, W. Va.: Patmos Press, 1981.

Yzermans, Vincent A. *All Things in Christ*. Westminster, Md.: Newman Press, 1954.

IV. Historical and General Sources

Acton, John. *Essays on Church and State*. New York: Thomas Y. Crowell Co., 1968.

_____. *Essays on Freedom and Power*. Cleveland: World Publishing Co., 1964.

———. *"The Vatican Council." North British Review* 53 (October 1870), 183–229.

Altholz, Josef. *The Liberal Catholic Movement and Its Contributors.* London: Burns and Oates, 1962.

Aubert, Roger. "Aspects divers du néo-Thomisme sous le Pontificat de Léon XIII." In *Aspetti Della Cultura Cattolica Nell'Eta di Leone XIII,* pp. 133–227. Rome: Edizioni 5 June, 1960.

———. "La Géographie ecclésiologique au XIXᵉ Siècle." In *L'Ecclésiologie au XIXᵉ Siècle,* edited by Maurice Nédoncelle. Unam Sanctam, No. 34, pp. 11–55. Paris: Editions du Cerf, 1960.

———. *Le Pontificat de Pie IX 1846–1878,* rev. ed. Paris: Bloud et Gay, 1963.

Beales, Arthur C. F. *Education under Penalty: English Catholic Education from the Reformation to the Fall of James II.* London: Athlone Press, 1963.

Bossy, John. *The English Catholic Community 1570–1850.* New York: Oxford University Press, 1976.

Bradbury, Malcolm, and James McFarlane, eds. *Modernism: 1890–1930.* New York: Penguin, 1976. Volume is part of series Pelican Guide to European Literature.

Bremond, Henri. *L'Histoire littéraire du sentiment religieux en France.* 11 vols. Paris: Bloud et Gay, 1916–1932.

Brown, James Baldwin. *An Historical Account of the Laws Enacted against Catholics in England and in Ireland.* London: Underwood and Blacks, 1913.

Burke, Bernard, and Ashworth P. Burke. "Petre." In *A Genealogical and Heraldic History of the Peerage and Baronetage, the Privy Council, Knightage and Companionage.* 76th edition. London: Harrison and Sons, 1914.

Butler, Charles. *Historical Memoires Respecting the English, Irish and Scottish Catholics from the Reformation to the Present Time.* London: John Murray, 1819.

Butler, Cuthbert. *The Vatican Council.* 2 vols. London: Longmans, Green, 1930.

Caraman, Philip. *The Other Face: Catholics under Elizabeth I.* London: Longmans, 1960.

———. *Years of Siege: Catholic Life, James I to Cromwell.* London: Longmans, 1966.

Chadwick, Owen. *The Secularization of the European Mind in the Nineteenth Century.* Cambridge: University Press, 1978.

_____. *The Victorian Church*. 2 vols. London: A. and C. Black, 1970.

The Church Teaches. Translated by John F. Clarkson, S.J., John H. Edwards, S.J., et al. St. Louis: B. Herder Book Co., 1955

Congar, Yves. "L'Ecclésiologie de la Révolution française au Concile du Vatican, sous le signe de l'affirmation de l'autorité." In *L'Ecclésiologie au XIXᵉ Siècle*, edited by Maurice Nédoncelle. Unam Sanctam, No. 34, pp. 77–114. Paris: Editions du Cerf, 1960.

Davies, D. R. *On to Orthodoxy*. New York: Macmillan, 1949.

Davies, Horton. *Worship and Theology in England*. 5 vols. Princeton: University Press, 1961.

Elliott, Walter. *The Life of Father Hecker*. New York: Columbus Press, 1891.

Ellis, John Tracy, ed. *Documents of American Catholic History*. 2 vols. Chicago: Henry Regnery, 1957.

Gladstone, William. *The Vatican Decrees in Their Bearing on Civil Allegiance*. In *Newman and Gladstone: The Vatican Decrees*, edited by Alvan Ryan, pp. 6–72. Notre Dame, Ind.: University of Notre Dame Press, 1962.

Gwynn, Denis. *A Hundred Years of Catholic Emancipation*. London: Longmans, Green, 1929.

_____. *The Struggle for Catholic Emancipation (1750–1829)*. London: Longmans, Green, 1928.

Harnack, Adolf. *What Is Christianity?* Translated by Thomas Bailey Saunders. Introduction by Rudolph Bultmann. New York: Harper Torchbook, 1957.

Havran, Martin. *The Catholics in Caroline England*. Stanford: University Press, 1962.

Hemphill, B. *The Early Vicars Apostolic of England 1685–1750*. London: Burns and Oates, 1954.

Hennesey, James J., S.J. *American Catholics*. New York: Oxford University Press, 1981.

_____. "National Traditions and the First Vatican Council." *Archivium Historicae Pontificiae* 7 (1969), 491–512.

_____. "Papacy and Episcopacy in Eighteenth and Nineteenth Century American Thought." *Records of the American Catholic Historical Society of Philadelphia* 77 (September 1966), 175–89.

Hocedez, Edgar, S.J. *Histoire de la Théologie au XIXᵉ Siècle*. Vol. II: *Epanouissement de la Théologie 1831–1870*. Brussels: L'Edition Universelle, 1952.

Holmes, J. Derek. *More Roman than Rome: English Catholicism in the Nineteenth Century*. London: Burns and Oates, 1978.

Hughes, Philip. *The Catholic Question 1685–1829*. London: Sheed and Ward, 1929.

————. *The Reformation in England*. New York: Macmillan, 1962.

Jones, Heribert, O.F.M. Cap. *Moral Theology*. Westminster, Md.: Newman Bookshop, 1951.

Latourette, Kenneth S. *The Nineteenth Century in Europe: Background and Roman Catholic Phase*. New York: Harper, 1958.

Leslie, Shane. *Henry Edward Manning: His Life and Labours*. New York: Kenedy, 1954.

McAvoy, Thomas. *The Great Crisis in American Catholic History 1895–1900*. Chicago: Henry Regnery, 1957.

McClelland, V. *Cardinal Manning: His Public Life and Influence*. London: Oxford Press, 1962.

McCool, Gerald. *Catholic Theology in the Nineteenth Century: The Quest for a Unitary Method*. New York: Seabury, 1977.

MacDougall, Hugh, O.M.I. *The Acton-Newman Relations: The Dilemma of Christian Liberalism*. New York: Fordham University Press, 1962.

McNabb, Vincent, O.P., ed. *The Decrees of the Vatican Council*. New York: Benziger, 1907.

Manning, Henry Edward. *Petri Privilegium*. London: Longmans, Green, 1871.

————. *The True Story of the Vatican Council*. London: Henry S. King, 1877.

————. *The Vatican Decrees in Their Bearing on Civil Allegiance*. New York: Catholic Publication Society, 1875.

Mansi, Johannes. *Sacrorum conciliorum nova et amplissima collectio*. Edited by L. Petit and J. B. Martin. Leipzig: Societé Nouvelle d'Edition de la Collection Mansi, 51 (1926), 430–50.

Marie Adelaide de Cicé. Translated by John Joyce, S.J. Paris: Les Presses Monastiques, 1962. No author given.

Mathew, David. *Catholicism in England 1535–1935*. London: Longmans, Green, 1936.

Nédoncelle, Maurice, ed. *L'Ecclésiologie au XIXᵉ Siècle*. Unam Sanctam, No. 34. Paris: Editions du Cerf, 1960.

Newman, John Henry. *Eight Lectures on the Position of Catholics in England*. London: Catholic Truth Society, 1890.

————. *Letter to the Duke of Norfolk*. In *Newman and Gladstone: The*

Vatican Decrees, edited by Alvan Ryan, pp. 75–228. Notre Dame, Ind.: University of Notre Dame Press, 1962.

Ott, Ludwig. *Fundamentals of Catholic Dogma.* St. Louis: B. Herder, 1954.

Purcell, Edward. *Life of Cardinal Manning.* 2 vols. New York: Macmillan, 1898.

Reardon, Bernard. *Liberalism and Tradition: Aspects of Catholic Thought in Nineteenth-Century France.* Cambridge: University Press, 1975.

Schleiermacher, Friedrich. *On Religion: Speeches to Its Cultured Despisers.* New York: Harper Torchbook, 1958.

Schoof, T. M. *A Survey of Catholic Theology 1800–1970.* Paramus, N.J.: Paulist Newman Press, 1970.

Smith, Warren Sylvester. *The London Heretics 1870–1914.* New York: Dodd, Mead, 1968.

"Society of the Daughters of the Heart of Mary: A Short Sketch." 1963. (A pamphlet; no place or publisher supplied.)

Spalding, John Lancaster. *Education and the Higher Life.* Chicago: A. C. McClure, 1890.

Sweeney, David, O.F.M. *The Life of John Lancaster Spalding.* New York: Herder and Herder, 1965.

Teilhard de Chardin, Pierre. *Building the Earth.* Wilkes-Barre, Pa.: Dimension, 1965.

Thureau-Dangin, Paul. *The English Catholic Revival in the Nineteenth Century.* 2 vols. London: Simpkin, 1914.

Tootell, Hugh. *Dodd's Church History of England.* 5 vols. London: Dolman, 1839.

Ward, Bernard. *The Dawn of Catholic Emancipation 1781–1803.* 2 vols. London: Longmans, Green, 1909.

————. *Eve of Catholic Emancipation 1803–1829.* 3 vols. London: Longmans, Green, 1911.

————. *Sequel to Catholic Emancipation.* 2 vols. New York: Longmans, Green, 1915.

Ward, Maisie. *Insurrection versus Resurrection.* New York: Sheed and Ward, 1937.

Ward, Wilfrid. *William George Ward and the Catholic Revival.* London: Macmillan, 1893.

Watkin, E. I. *Roman Catholicism in England from the Reformation to 1950.* London: Oxford University Press, 1957.

White, Antonia. *The Hound and the Falcon.* London: Collins-Fontana, 1965.

V. Special Sources

Clutton, Sir George (nephew of Maude Petre). Letters from London: December 10, 1969 and March 17, 1970.

Keenan, Agnes (Assistant-General, Society of the Daughters of the Heart of Mary). Letter from Paris: March 18, 1971.

Louis-David, Anne. Interviews at her home in Paris: October 22, 24, 1970.

Merewether, Mrs. Cally. Interview at her home in London: November 22, 1970.

Pirenne, Mrs. Maurice (niece of Maude Petre). Interview at her home in Oxford: November 10, 1970.

Sexton, Eileen (Superior, Society of the Daughters of the Heart of Mary, St. Elizabeth's Center, Gramercy Park, New York City). Interview at St. Elizabeth's Center: January 15, 1971.

Vidler, Alec. Interview at his home in Rye, England: October 8, 1970.

Watson, S. M. (English Provincial, Society of the Daughters of the Heart of Mary). Letter from London: April 7, 1971.

White, Antonia. Letter from London: March 27, 1971.

VI. Obituary Accounts of Maude Petre

Times (London), December 17, 1942, p. 1.

Times (London), December 19, 1942, p. 6.

Times Literary Supplement, January 2, 1943, p. 7.

Index